the Gospel of Yudas

PRAISE FOR *HANGWOMAN*

'Meera is at her best when she examines the lives of her women characters . . . The writing is strong . . . An epic novel'—*Outlook*

'A daring book, for the panoramic sweep of its canvas, for the sheer audacity of its narrative logic . . . for its irreverent play with the paradoxes of life—Love and Death'—*The Hindu*

'This striking novel includes within its majestic sweep the enigmas of the human condition . . . Stunning images bring out the depth and intensity of Chetna's spiritual development, and stand testimony to the author's consummate writing style'—*Deccan Herald*

'Meera achieves a vision of [Kolkata] that is both acutely observed, almost anthropological, in its minute detailing and, at the same time, mythic in its evocation of the city's decaying, decrepit majesty . . . One of the most extraordinary accomplishments in recent Indian fiction'—*Indian Express*

'An absorbing novel'—*New Indian Express*

'One of the strongest voices in contemporary Malayalam literature . . . Meera plays with the reader's anticipation masterfully . . . The novel is extremely atmospheric . . . Meera turns the entire city into a haunted house'—*Open*

'The book heaves with violence, is lush with metaphor and shocks with details. The reader can only gasp at the surgical precision with which Meera describes the act of hanging'—*The Hindu Business Line*

'An immense, intense coiled rope of a novel . . . There are chillingly clear-eyed vignettes and moments of razor-sharp dark humour . . . If *Aarachar*, the original, was—plot, stock and barrel—"Malayalam's ultimate gift of love to Bengal," as its translator J. Devika puts it, its English translation is no less a bonus for showing us, its non-Malayali, non-Bengali readership, the dazzling interstices of her story, instantly recognisable across time and space'—*India Today*

'An incisive critique of the barbarism of the death penalty . . . [The book] gives us a glimpse into the inner lives of those who have been deputed to execute it through generations . . . A vast and riveting sweep of time, locked into the gritty interstices of the contemporary—a pastiche made of fact and fiction, news bulletins and nightmares'—*Mint*

'Stunning . . . Meera weaves history, romance and the politics of the present together into a narrative of incredible complexity . . . J. Devika's translation is superb, and she captures the rich detail of Meera's Malayalam: descriptive, textured and evocative . . . Reading Meera, in Devika's meticulous and inspired translation, we experience the author's spectacular ventriloquism. And we are also reminded of the tradition that Meera comes from, which she has burnished and transcended with her epic novel'—*Caravan*

PRAISE FOR *YELLOW IS THE COLOUR OF LONGING*

'Interesting, challenging'—Mahasweta Devi

'[Meera's] stories cover an amazing range, and in each her idiom is inseparable from the plots and characters . . . Each story invokes the inner violence of contemporary society in Kerala'—*Caravan*

'One of the most powerful voices in contemporary Malayalam writing'—*Mint*

'A literary heavyweight'—*Indian Express*

the Gospel of Yudas

K.R. MEERA

Translated from the Malayalam by
Rajesh Rajamohan

HAMISH HAMILTON
an imprint of
PENGUIN BOOKS

HAMISH HAMILTON
Published by the Penguin Group
Penguin Books India Pvt. Ltd, 7th Floor, Infinity Tower C, DLF Cyber City,
Gurgaon 122 002, Haryana, India
Penguin Group (USA) Inc., 375 Hudson Street, New York, New York 10014, USA
Penguin Group (Canada), 90 Eglinton Avenue East, Suite 700, Toronto,
Ontario, M4P 2Y3, Canada
Penguin Books Ltd, 80 Strand, London WC2R 0RL, England
Penguin Ireland, 25 St Stephen's Green, Dublin 2, Ireland (a division of
Penguin Books Ltd)
Penguin Group (Australia), 707 Collins Street, Melbourne, Victoria 3008, Australia
Penguin Group (NZ), 67 Apollo Drive, Rosedale, Auckland 0632, New Zealand
Penguin Books (South Africa) (Pty) Ltd, Block D, Rosebank Office Park,
181 Jan Smuts Avenue, Parktown North, Johannesburg 2193, South Africa

Penguin Books Ltd, Registered Offices: 80 Strand, London WC2R 0RL, England

First published in Malayalam as 'Yudasinte Suvisesham' in *Meerayude
Novellakal* by DC Books, Kottayam 2014
First published in Hamish Hamilton by Penguin Books India 2016

Copyright © K.R. Meera 2016
English translation copyright © Rajesh Rajamohan 2016

ISBN 9780670088584

Typeset in Adobe Caslon Pro by Manipal Digital Systems, Manipal
Printed at Replika Press Pvt. Ltd, India

A PENGUIN RANDOM HOUSE COMPANY

CONTENTS

the Gospel of Yudas

A traitor can never sleep. His hunger is eternal; his thirst, insatiable. The burning inside his body won't be doused even if he immerses himself in water. No matter how hard he tries to drown himself in alcohol, he still remains intensely conscious.

These were the lessons I learned from the life of Crocodile 'Croc' Yudas. Diving to recover dead bodies was his vocation. Every village had someone whose job it was to dredge corpses from the deep. In our lake, dead bodies raced among themselves daily to find their way to the surface. So 'Croc' Yudas had no respite. As soon as he brought a body to the shore, he'd collect his wages and walk off to the moonshine joint. There, he'd drink to the brink only to saunter back to the lake in complete control of his wits and submerge himself up to his neck in the water. On the lake's shore, hemmed in by the valley where violet butterworts and brown-eyed droseras bloomed, he had a windowless shack that looked like a morgue. Below the flight of stones near the shore, where he'd land the cadavers, womenfolk would gather in the afternoons, their skirts hitched above their breasts, the fabric hugging their wet bodies as they washed clothes or scraped skin with *incha*-scrubbers while bathing. It was during these afternoons that he took classes for boys on the art of lovemaking.

In those times dead bodies surfaced in the lake face down. I don't know how it happens now. The pale lifeless bodies would rock about on the lake's turgid green, heaving surface like a stalk of plantain or a white crocodile. 'Croc' Yudas would glide towards the shore with the corpse as his float. Gasping for air, he'd beach the body, its bottom half still lying in the water, and perch upon the washers' rock to light up a ganja beedi. When he emerged from the lake, his ashen body would turn a morbid blue. The smoke from the joint would cast a strange light around him. He'd poke at the corpse with his left leg to turn its face around for the benefit of the cops. 'I bumped him off,' he'd announce proudly. 'Write this one on me.' The officers would ignore his words, provoking him to reel off a volley of abuse: 'Pay heed, you mongrels! Long Live the Revolution! Naxalbari Zindabad! Arrest me if you dare!'

Nobody paid much attention to him. Except me.

The year was 1985. Although I was only a five-year-old when the Emergency was declared—an event of which I had no grasp or memory—and Indira Gandhi had called it off a long time ago, the state of emergency continued in my home. Commands like 'Less talk, more work!', or 'Discipline makes a great nation!' glared at me in the face. I was not permitted to laugh or play with other children from the time I was a little kid. I dreamed every day of a Naxal who would have the audacity to liberate me. In our feudal home—our *Naalukettu*—before I went to sleep in my room under the yellowed ceiling made of Anjiliwood, I'd chant silently, 'Naxalbari Zindabad!' Every time the cattle twitched their legs in the stable, or the haystacks moved, I would await his arrival with bated breath. But my ardent chanting didn't help! No Naxalite ever came. Nobody annihilated the fascist machinery that smothered me. The amorous hormones in my body clamoured to take on fascism. I couldn't be in love with anyone less than a Naxalite.

In the beginning, 'Croc' Yudas had not featured even in my wildest dreams. Yet it happened, just like that.

But this story will not be about my love. Stories of love and tears have always made me puke. This will not be the story of the revolution either. That has already been told many times over. This is going to be the story of cadavers. Be warned! When the corpses swimming face down like crocodiles were turned over, their faces, nibbled at by the fish, would give one a cardiac arrest.

ONE

My father was a policeman in the police
corps' camp at Kakkayam. He quit the
job when the Emergency was withdrawn.
Thereafter, the old man's custodial torture
routines were trained on us at home—mother
and her three children. His hands never had
their fill of vocational savagery. Wanting more,
he would kick me around like a soccer ball
having tied my feet and arms in a single knot.
But he couldn't sleep either. During his daily
drink binges, he regurgitated the fond old tales
of brutal torture from his camp over the pickle.
We were to stand in attention and listen to him
repeat the bloody tales of his butchery on the
inmates at the camp lock-up. Thus I'd known
K. Rajan, P. Rajan, Cheria Rajan and Rajan
the rubber tapper since my childhood. Cheria

Rajan was found dead in a school building. Every time he recalled Cheria Rajan's story, my father would let out a hiss as though his tongue just got seared by a spicy fish curry: Ishhhh . . .

It wasn't long before tremors from Parkinson's disease struck my father down. Unable to move, he lived the rest of his life trapped in our house. Amma's cousin moved in soon after, ostensibly to help us out. But like traitors, paramours too could never sleep. They too wouldn't be able to laugh or hold their heads high.

Whatever . . .

It was my father who identified Yudas at the shore. 'This is Das . . . isn't he?' he asked of Yudas in a trembling voice.

Yudas's visage suddenly turned pale, like a dead man. I too was dumbstruck. That night Yudas fled from our village.

Earlier that day, my father and I had gone to identify the body of his nephew at the lake. The boy had drowned, and Yudas had to dive and recover his body. The boy, Balu, was one of the students at Yudas's classes on the art of lovemaking. It was from him that I came to know about those classes. He was a nice lad. He used to like me a lot. I couldn't forget how he'd lean on a column to watch me comb and plait my hair in the little mirror on the wall while rain poured into the open central courtyard of the Naalukettu. One day he gathered enough courage to plant a kiss on the nape of my neck. I turned around to glare at him. Our ages were the same. Cornered by my glare, his courage drained instantly. Afterwards he begged me for forgiveness. I felt funny when he confessed to me, in tears, that it was Yudas who'd taught him that kissing a woman' neck would render her defenceless.

'What else did he teach you?'

I interrogated Balu under the mango tree in the south end of our courtyard with the curiosity of a fifteen-year-old.

'I can't tell you any of that, Prema . . .'

'What about those bodies from the lake . . . how does he find them?'

'He never says anything about that.'

'Isn't he scared when he dives deep into the lake?'

'Who knows? He only talks about undead women and their bodies.'

'Does he kiss the nape of dead women's necks too?'

Flustered, Balu looked at me. 'You must forgive me, Prema!'

'I never thought you'd behave like this.'

'Please don't tell anyone.'

'I won't. But I do want to have a word with that man . . .'

'Prema, please don't . . .'

'I will, so long as I am Prema!'

In the afternoon, as soon as my mother settled down for her siesta and my younger brothers went away frolicking, I sneaked out of the house from the south end of the yard. I leapt across the fence and sprinted along the valley towards the lake. In those times, crossing the pebble-strewn valley didn't require much effort. All you had to do was hitch your long skirt higher at the top of the ridge and let yourself go in a free fall. Like a bouncy ball, you would ricochet past the mounds and roll in the wind until you finally reached the shore. That day when I arrived at the desolate shore, drenched with the dusky sunlight, I was out of breath. The immense bluish lake lay before me, stretching beyond the limits of my vision.

I couldn't find Yudas there. The hedgerows in the valley had had a harvest of white gooseberries and wild red strawberries. I marched towards his shack, dragging along my white skirt printed with blue flowers. There I saw him weeping as he lay on the ocherous floor built from sand and dirt. I was only fifteen then; the cries of grown men hadn't begun to make me laugh yet. If anything, his tears melted my heart. I looked at him as I fiddled with a pebble that protruded from the yellowing wall. The lake billowed lazily, about a stone's throw away behind me. He stood up with a start, perhaps because my shadow blocked the light. Tugging at my plaits, I waited in terror. When I asked him the reason why he cried, he frowned and chided me for showing up at his place. That was it. I lost my temper.

'You taught Balu filthy stuff! Why?' I inquired boldly. 'He tried to be dirty with me . . . And you made him do it . . . I am going to tell on you . . . I'll tell everyone.'

His face turned slightly pale, as he recognized the sincerity in my threat.

'Chhi!'

He reacted angrily at nobody in particular.

'Go right ahead. Tell on me. I am not afraid of anyone.'

'Me neither!'

'Get away from my face!'

'What if I don't?'

The breeze from the lake had begun to unfurl my long skirt like an umbrella. I scooped it up to sit on my knees. Then I chanted, 'Naxalbari Zindabad!'

His face turned red and in that moment he seemed vulnerable and delicate like a timid fifth grader. I was certain then that he was a Naxal who'd been hiding in our hamlet.

'What do you want?'

I had a smile on my face. 'Teach me how to swim.'

He kept peering at me. He had languorous eyes. His hair was bronzed and overgrown. The teardrops on his scarlet-speckled beard and moustache gleamed. Suddenly, I had a crush on him.

'Teach swimming? To a girl?'

'Not just swimming. You have to teach me how to dive and recover dead bodies too'

It took him a while to rein in his rage. Then he stood up, rubbing hard on his beard and moustache.

'Girl, you should go back home.'

'I am going to tell everyone what Balu said.'

'I've already told you not to intimidate me. I am not scared of anything in life any more.'

'Me neither!'

'You are a pest! What in the world do you want?'

'Where do you get the grit to touch a dead human?'

He suddenly became stiff as if he'd just been slapped on his face.

'Aren't you scared when you swim up to a corpse?' I continued. 'What crosses your mind when you look at a dead face?'

He was seething with anger and his face betrayed a smidgeon of anguish at having been humiliated unexpectedly.

'Get lost, you scamp!' he yelled.

I too was stubborn. 'I am not going anywhere until you agree to teach me how to swim'

We confronted each other. He called me names. Enraged, I hurled my plaits around and challenged him. If he wasn't going to teach me, then watch out, I would do it myself. Tugging at the hem of my skirt, I ran towards the lake. I could hear him curse over the wind—'Damn you girl, you mean nothing to me. I couldn't care less if you were dead.' Yet when I fell into the shoal with a splash, I saw him run to the doorstep. I turned to watch him as I dipped deeper into the water, dragging my long skirt further into the mud and leafless water plants. The lake turned into a husband waiting for his bride. I fell in love with it. The water had a strange warmth as it held me in a sensuous thrall. My white skirt with blue flower prints bobbed momentarily above the water like an umbrella before I submitted myself to the surge and it began to wash me away. When the water pulled me towards the deep end of the outer lake, I stood upright straddling the waves. The lake held me up.

That was a weird experience. I was frolicking with abandon along the green layer of water in the middle of the lake. The sky above was a clear blue. A school of lovesick white pearl fish tapped my hands. Chromides bit my ankles lustily. I wanted to cry. Freedom was luring me.

'Naxalbari Zindabad.' I chanted for no reason. 'Long Live the Revolution. Comrade Varghese Zindabad.'

Momentarily, I spread my arms amid the waves as if they were my wings and I began to plummet towards the lake's bottom. Like 'Croc' Yudas, I dived deeper into the water. 'As deep as possible,' I commanded myself with a fifteen-year-old's spunk. I had heard that the blood-red, gooey mud at the bottom of the lake had magnetic power. Once you were trapped in its field, you couldn't escape. There was another lake boiling underneath the bed of this one. I wanted to get there. The upper lake tried to stop me. But I refused to give up. I plunged intractably into the dense water like a chromide with plaited hair. My heart began to stir as I neared the bottom. I craved for water like a fish thrown out of it. Sometimes I felt as though I was a baby jostling to get out of its mother's womb. At other times I was a combatant waging a revolution all by myself.

When I think about that experience after all these years, my mind unveils the myriad colours of the lake. The shimmering green above the rim of my eyes that turned to grey as I sank. The pale yellow when I swooped in. The orange of the ravenous depths where I sank and didn't exhale. The deep red that shone brightly as one descended deeper and touched down at the bed of the lake . . . The vision had me mesmerized and terrified at the same time.

My eyes were closed as I held my breath one more time. When I opened them again, I was startled to find someone lying straight and serene on his back with his arms tucked under his head on the reddened mud on the lake bed. His eyes were open and disdainful. I began to bawl in fear. Water filled my mouth and I couldn't breathe. The shock had me toss around at the bottom like a pearl fish. I began to lose consciousness when water entered my lungs. I saw him one more time before I passed out. Having been underwater for a long time, his face was white and swollen. His body was incandescent as though there was a lamp lighting him up from behind his head. For a moment I thought it was an illusion. A thousand chromides darted in all directions from his gut. I was certain it was a corpse. I felt suffocated in the unbearable light that emanated from the red silt and thick slimy green algae. I closed my eyes. My memory flapped its open gills like a pearl fish out of the water before it became still.

When I opened my eyes, I was lying along the edge of a cot in Yudas's cabin as though I were a wet skirt hung out to dry. My head drooped from the cot and when I tried to get up, water spilled out of my petticoat with a pearl fish in it. In stupor I watched it heave about on the dirt floor. 'Croc' Yudas bent down, scooped up the fish and threw it out of sight. I smiled when it fell in the lake. I whispered to him: 'Long Live the Revolution.' 'Croc' Yudas was alarmed. I gazed at him upside down. He too was soaking wet. He had striking features that I couldn't explain. He was not like any other men I knew. I sat up slowly and smiled once more. Then I chanted, 'Long Live the Naxalbari.'

'What did you say?' He looked at me in dismay. His body shook involuntarily. He stood next to me and lifted my face with his hands.

I saw teardrops swell in his turbid eyes that looked like two murky sediment-laden lakes.

'Total Revolution Is Our Goal, Future Generations Belong to Us!' I said.

He looked at me in panic. 'How old are you?' he enquired.

'Down with Fascism!' I continued. Watching him panic made me laugh. I leaned on his chest impulsively. He shivered with an icy chill.

'Please go home,' he begged.

'Kiss me,' I commanded.

He glanced at me in trepidation. Despite my exhaustion, it made me giggle.

'You're the one teaching boys how to kiss girls, aren't you?'

'But I . . . I've never . . .'

He was blushing crimson. It was funny. He was almost twice my age. I watched him become bashful with curiosity, and stood up gallantly. Water continued to drip from my forehead. His bewildered countenance made me bolder. I was learning about the alliance of fear and assault; rebellion and victory. There must be something in everyone's heart that is hard to find, as though its limbs have been tied to a grindstone at the bottom of the lake. I sat leaning against his chest. Water from the river drained off our bodies, intermingling as it flowed to the floor. With my half-closed eyes, I could see the rousing tingle coursing through our hands as if tiny grains of sediments were being stirred up by deep-water fish reposing in their camouflage.

Perhaps it was then that Balu walked in. Neither Yudas nor I knew.

'Please go home.' He continued the pleading, 'Do not touch me. Don't ever love me. Prema, you have no idea who I am!'

'You are my Naxalite. Please rescue me. Let's run away to Pulpally? Or Andhra? How about Bengal?'

I too pleaded with him. He tried to push me away. But I held him tight.

'Let's run away. The world needs us. Our love. Sacrifice. Our blood . . .'

'I am a sinner. You shouldn't love me!'

'I will love you. I will always love you. You are my Naxalite.'

He pushed me away with a whimper. However, the fire in his chest stayed in mine.

I felt for him the same yearning that a fish has for water. I took his face, soaked with tears and lake water, in my palms.

'There is blood on my hands,' he said in a muffled voice. 'These hands have touched countless dead people.'

'You can't scare me with stories of blood and dead bodies.'

'You are only a little girl.'

'Well, I am more mature than you are.'

I smiled again and planted the tenderest kiss I could possibly conjure on his cheek. I caressed his beard and stroked the copper strands before I pulled away from him in tears.

'I will come again,' I declared.

Afterwards I left Yudas, shaking the edge of the long skirt long dried from the steam of our embrace, my wet hair unfurled. I scampered back home, splashing water over *sikerpud* bushes with their little spittoons, and the droseras waiting to snare ants in their gum-laced leaf traps. The sun had begun to wane. The wafting lyre from the hills across the shore had begun to unwind. Womenfolk hauling linens had begun to arrive at the lake, past the valley, to wash the dirt off their clothes and their bodies. I stopped at the bend hidden by the butterworts' hedge. Behind the thicket of wild raspberries, on top of the laterite stones that looked like dark-brown coral reef, Balu waited for me. He looked at me with the reproachful eyes of the betrayed. I skipped across the bend as if nothing had happened.

'I will die, Prema!' he called out from behind.

I turned around to see him. 'Why not! Die,' I said nonchalantly.

The tears that welled up in his eyes made me laugh. I didn't look back as I rushed to climb the steep ascent from the lake towards my house.

Balu vanished after that. The next day his dead body showed up. It was then that my father identified Yudas, once he landed the dead body at the shore, and the villagers learned who he really was. In the end Yudas left the village, leaving behind the nip of lake water and the warmth of blood in my heart.

After all these long years the only regret I ever had was this: the corpse I saw at the bottom of the lake—it never came to the surface.

TWO

In his heyday, my father wouldn't regurgitate the old tales of blood and gore without burning incense and bellowing 'BLOODY ROTTEN SCUM OF AN ASS-IMPALER!'

My father had given up the job of a cop out of disappointment when the fearsome Kakkayam camp was shut down. Having worked at that camp, he believed working in an everyday police station would be as degrading and abominable as shrinking a tiger into a cat. After voluntary retirement he spent day and night boozing at home. He'd boast about the drinking binges of his colleagues at the camp and how the bottles of liquor piled up into a hill as tall as the Eeppan hill in our village. The human flesh wasted by third-degree torture chambers filled the camp and incense had to be burned to overpower the putrid stench. The fragrance from the incense sticks would make him sprightly. Those sticks of incense were testament to the grotesque desire for power among gods and humans alike. If there was no one to plead mercy, there would be no joy for God or man in dispensing their sovereign rule.

In our feudal home, the visitor's area was filled with thick white smoke as if wet raw wood was being burned in the gloom of the rooms. In the dense cloud rising from the smouldering incense sticks, my father would lie in an old wooden lounge chair, staring with his round eyes that looked like two hanging stones about to pop out. As soon as there was a mention of the police, he became possessed. Tugging hard at my mother's or my hair, he would yell:

'BLOODY ROTTEN SCUM OF AN ASS-IMPALER! You have no idea what khaki means! It is not a goddamned piece of cloth! It is an emotion, a state of mind, an ideology, an article of faith . . .'

My father twirled his moustache as he stared me down.

'What do you even know about the police? We could accomplish anything we wanted. You haven't been to Kakkayam, have you? The remotest of remote settlements. Nothing more than a hillock. What do you think happened? We transformed that place overnight. Oh! You don't know, do you? Yes. Ho! We've got wireless, telescope and police dogs to top it all off. It was all a celebration—a grand show of festivity.'

By the time I was ten years old, I had memorized it all.

'Tell me now. Where was the camp's head office?' my father roared as he grabbed me by my neck. He was going to strangle me to death any moment now.

'Kuttiyaa—' I would begin to blurt out the location of the head office in mortal fear.

'Bah! Bloody rotten bitch! How many times have I told you! The first camp was in the inspection bungalow's recreation club. We moved out a little later.'

He would help himself another shot of liquor, jiggle the towel tied around his head a little, dart fingers about his thighs to scratch a bit before he began to pace up and down in the room filled with the cloud of smoke. Soon he would begin retelling the pastoral beauty around the inspection bungalow, the terrifying solitude of the Kakkayam dam and the Konippara mountain watching over it like a sentry, piling on the seclusion and terror.

'Do you hear me, you little imp? Whenever we had an inmate crouched over so that we could clobber his backbone to smithereens, the sound of each blow echoed right back to us from the mountain, crashing on to the powerhouse. You get it? That was as good as it got. It warms the cockles of my heart every time I think of it. The sound of the waterfall. Eerie nights taken over by the creepy cries of a million crickets. The howling wind. Oh! *That* was what policing was all about. That was what it meant to wear the uniform. Truly a golden age!' My father would wipe his teary eyes and then say, 'Now, where did we get the pestle rod?'

He was at my throat again.

'Thoma—' I would stammer.

'Start with the initial,' he thundered.

'P.J. Thomas,' I spewed it out like a parrot. He was an employee at the powerhouse who lived close to the camp. The pestle rod had been brought from his kitchen. The camp was about a kilometre from the inspection bungalow. It used to be an old workshop surrounded by three bivouacs. Armed sentries manned the building. The quarter in the west led into a sprawling room where Parameswaran *Saar* and other top cops had their office. The fan brought from the bungalow ran all the time in that room.

'Now tell me the name of the police dog in our camp?'

'Shanti.'

'Ah!'

My father would let me go, relieved that I could finally answer a question.

'I should have named you after Shanti. It dawned on me only a little later. Ho! You haven't seen her, have you? She was something!'

I would rub my bleary eyes and stare at him vengefully. My younger brothers were already halfway through their sleep. My mother yawned drowsily, grinding her teeth to mute curse words, while I strained to overcome the pain and angst by envisioning again the siege of Kaayanna police station. I was there with the thirteen rebels led by K. Venu. That was me among them, with a ponytail, wearing a long skirt and a blouse with puffed sleeves. Repeating to the captain: 'I will stand up to anything. I am not scared of anyone. My body, I pledge it to the world. My mind, I pledge it to mankind. Ugh!' Despairing: 'If only the comrade could've helped himself with more weapons . . . He should've given a musket or two to his fellow fighters, been more careful with the kerosene lamp when it tipped over. Even better, he should've fallen over to shut out the fire with his own body before it began to blaze. He could've given an answer to this rotten world wallowing in darkness.'

Unbeknownst to the schemes of rebellion in my mind, my father would continue to brag:

'You've got to work in the police force if you ever want to do a real job. Whack the hell out of people. Roll them up. Ha! Rolling them up. That's what you call a real duty. The kind only *real* men like Parameswaran Saar and I could do. It was *bodies* we were rolling up, not wheat dough. Live human bodies! What is a human body? A bit of skin, some flesh and bones.

Listen to me, you little brat! Do you have any idea how many men had their bones pulled right out of them with these very hands?

'When you rolled them up, the inmates' machismo would be torn apart,' my father continued, letting out a chilling roar. 'The men would cry. They would sweat in agony. Those who administer the pain sweat too. And as the pain grows so does the hardness of their perspiration. Salt. Salt from the sweat. It drips all over the floor and on their own bodies and then it dries and forms scabs. The skin slithers from the body, blood oozes out, and the flesh begins to crack and fall off. By now they are ready to admit to anything.' Father twirled his handlebar moustache as he glared at me and said, 'What do you all know? We made them throw up even the mother's milk they had when they were little babies.'

When I look back and think about Yudas after all these years, I understand how my father's homage to the torture camp could stir my own infatuation and adoration for Yudas. Only a subject of brutality like me would be able to recognize Yudas, the benevolent vanquisher.

Yet, who was he? No Das ever appeared in my father's stories.

When my father called his name out at the shore as Yudas pulled up Balu's body, the people around us gawked at him. Das who? 'He is Das, the fourteenth insurgent, isn't he?' My father queried, shaking all over. Years of addiction to alcohol and ill health had diminished my father into no more than a skeleton.

Yudas raged like a smouldering fire poked out of ashes. His mouth and nose reeked of marijuana.

'I am not Das!' he yelled as he lunged towards Father. *I am Yudas. Judas, the betrayer. He that is faithful in that which is least faithful also in much.*' He grabbed the rattling skeleton that was my father and shook him wildly. *'He who is cowardly with only a little is cowardly also in much.'* I really thought the violent shaking would end my father's life right then. For a moment I hoped he would throw my father's weakened body into the deep end of the lake. Had the mob around them not intervened, it could've happened. Yudas suddenly let go of my father who tottered about and struggled to regain balance. He pulled Balu's body with manic force on to the shore where it fell with a thud. Then he turned back and he threw himself on to the expanse of the lake like a fishing net. The swelling water soared as it made way for his abrupt departure, washing Balu's body back and forth in the water like a plantain stalk. I would never forget Balu's face. Chromides had nibbled it into a pitted human coral. I took great care to burn numerous incense sticks when his body was taken home, draped in white sheets and laid on the floor for funeral rituals. My father sat looking at him keenly, his head quivering. I was thinking again of Yudas while Balu's mother, my aunt, wailed. Yudas too was crying as he swam back into the lake and vanished out of sight.

I racked my brain trying to figure out who Yudas could be. Thirteen of them had laid siege to the police station. There had been no Das. I don't recall my father ever mentioning a nickname for Apputty or Little Rajan or Pushparajan or even Bharathan that sounded anything like Das. Who, then, was Das? I had to find the answer to that question. I was thinking tenderly of the fourteenth rebel who couldn't find a place in history. The more I thought about it, my love for him grew. When Balu's body was lowered into the funeral pit in the south end of our yard, I was watching the lake. In my heart my passion for Yudas surged. Light began to fade in the dusk and a dense green hue adorned the lake. I yearned to feel his pale face in my hands, caress the crimson shimmer in his long hair, and the overgrown, unkempt beard and moustache that made him look like Jesus Christ. I kept gazing at the middle of the lake. Could he be still lying immersed in the lake? I remembered how frantic his face had seemed. His eyes were bloodshot. His crimson-streaked hair was wet and glued to his scalp. He had unleashed a wild force in the waves when he swam away for the last time, which made me wobble and trip up although the water was only ankle-deep where I stood. Night fell on the lake while I kept my vigil, followed by the arrival of the moon. The water shone bright in the moonlight. Longing for his love, I looked everywhere for a glimpse of Yudas's shadow.

It was only after visiting the abandoned hut the next day that I was certain that Yudas was gone forever. The shack had been left open. Its interior was bare but for a small desk and a makeshift cot. All the other belongings—mud-stained clothes and towels and the little chest were gone. I stood there feeling an inexplicable loss. I didn't know what to do for a while. Fearing for the worst, I wondered if I would ever get another chance to escape from my bleak world. I would've loved him with all my heart, adored him and set out on the path of revolution. At fifteen, for the first time in my life, I endured the pangs of lost love, separation and the emptiness of letting go as I trudged the long walk home.

My father's condition had worsened by nightfall. He let the doctor know that he was knocked around violently by Yudas the day before. The doctor wondered why anyone would do such a thing. My father smiled at him with his trembling head and said: 'That son of a bitch! I'd tortured the shit out of him. Even the roller bent when I put him under it. He wouldn't say a word in the beginning. But I made him sing. He crooned whatever he knew by the time we broke his rib cage, just like a canary. Thanks to him, we dumped two of his mates in the gorge.'

In the porch beyond the half-walled entrance of my house, stalks of plantain with incense sticks stuck in them were strewn around behind Balu's head. The sight seared my heart. I began to have a recurring nightmare in which I flailed about in the deep end of the lake while my legs went limp. Many corpses lying with arms folded at the bottom beamed at me. All of them had Yudas's visage.

THREE

I met Yudas again on the banks of the River Kallai, far north from my village, but not until five years later.

I was in Kozhikode, attending college for a postgraduate diploma certificate. It was a novel branch of education at the time. Hitting the road to Kozhikode was my way of being as far away from home as possible. Until then, each year, I had expected Yudas to turn up any day. I would wake up every morning looking at the lake and thinking that the minutest speck on the surface could turn out to be him.

My father's situation had become miserable. Mother passed away, drowning in the lake. It happened while I was at the college hostel. That day my younger brother had hollered, looking for Mother, but she didn't respond because she wasn't home. In the evening, chromide hunters at the lake caught her long hair. They pulled out her blistered body as though it was a giant chromide hidden amidst the crevasses in the mud. With the exception of our enormous dilapidated Naalukettu, Amma's cousin, the illicit lover, had taken away all our properties. Father remained in the house stuck in his bed. I rarely visited home.

Those were awfully difficult days for me. I felt like a rubber doll tossed into the water, floating, bobbing up and down, finding neither its destiny, nor giving me peace of mind. I thought of Yudas every night. His memory agonized me the more I thought of him. Sometimes I hated him. I didn't think he really deserved my love because he gave himself up after being subjected to torture by my father. He was a coward. He put up nothing but deception. But wasn't I deceiving myself as well? Didn't I blow everything out of proportion to create a hero out of a coward? It was my fault. Love was an absurd emotion, especially if it was meant for a man. What was really needed was love for humanity. I felt guilty of violating the purity of my mind, having fallen for the wrong kind of love during the best period of my life. To atone for this, my mind returned to Kakkayam camp perpetually, submitting myself to the torture sessions which my father celebrated. I bit my teeth and pursed lips as I imagined yelling 'Victory for the Revolution' or 'Power to the Naxalbari'. Such whimsical illusions were all that remained in my generation. Everything else had vanished. My father's generation rolled up and down to rid themselves of my generation's bravery and grit to love, trust and fight. I prayed ardently to reclaim the strength to at least have trust. But no, my generation can never believe unless they feel the gashes from the nails with their bare hands.

I went to the river along with the rest of the students from my class when the news of a classmate's death by drowning broke out in school. He had participated in an agitation opposing the pollution of the River Chaliyaar. Later on there were rumours suggesting that this might have been the reason he was killed. It didn't really bother me much. Someone was dead. Someone had killed. That's all there was to it. But when I heard that the body had not yet been found, I was reminded of our lake. I felt nauseous standing at the edge of the wide river. A wave of memories rose in my mind. Many in the crowd took to boats and canoes in search for the body. Suddenly a man emerged from below the surface of the water with a dead body as though he were a heron breaking out of the river after catching a flapping pearl fish. Water sprayed everywhere. The man transferred the body to the boat and swam back into the river. I recognized him from the first glimpse. My heart skipped a beat. I held myself back having begun to yell 'Yudas!' I wondered if he'd announced 'Long Live the Revolution' when he was done! Did he holler 'Naxalbari Zindabad' or dare them with the jibe 'Arrest me if you have the nerve?' Did I hear him say that? I was too far away to see or hear him clearly. I wanted to throw myself into the river and swim up to him. As I looked on he vanished beyond the waves.

Standing there, I felt let down being a woman. In that moment I loved Yudas with a greater intensity than I had when I was a fifteen-year-old. While walking with the group headed to the dead boy's home, I thought about Yudas. He was lost from a distance. His crimson-streaked hair, a pale face and melancholic, languid eyes had flown away in the river. The wailing mother of the dead boy looked like my paternal aunt. It must have been a long time since I had last seen or even heard about someone whose life was claimed by water. After a long time, I inhaled the smoke from the incense. I saw the whitish toes of the feet swollen by water when we put a wreath on the dead body. An afternoon spent swimming in a lake, precipitated under a blue sky, haunted me. I knew I had to meet Yudas. Suddenly, my resentment for him evaporated. I was anxious to find where he had gone beyond the river. Even after all my classmates had left I hung around, as though I had swallowed the hook from a fishing rod. I wandered around for a long time on the shore. In the end I found his place. He lived by the far end of the river in a shanty cobbled out of coconut leaves. I entered his shack after washing my feet, soiled by all the tramping I had done along the muddy shoreline and in the river itself. I was exhausted.

He was drinking. Seeing me in his house startled him. But he didn't smile until he finished what was left in the bottle. I couldn't even utter a word as I fought the emotions raging within my mind. I clutched the bag hanging from my shoulder, tugged at the edge of my sari and stared at him with a sweaty face. He got up slowly to pull off a shirt from the wall, and did the buttons one by one before turning towards me.

'You must be Prema?'

His voice was lifeless. My voice was stuck in my throat. Yet my heart was overjoyed to know that he recognized me after five years.

'What are you doing here, Prema?' he asked in a flat even tone. My voice failed to come out. After a long time I asked him what he was doing there.

Yudas smiled apologetically. 'I have been living in the area for a while now. I do think about your village sometimes. I think of you too. I even thought of paying a visit once. But I fell sick when I was about to start. How could I then? You have seen for yourself. I am busy here every day. Someone will die drowning each day.' He spoke about this and that as though we'd met for a routine conversation. My heart was pounding. I couldn't take my eyes off him. Yudas, 'Croc' Yudas. The revolutionary who'd recovered corpses from my lake. The champion of my liberation struggle.

'Come inside,' he invited. The room reeked of ganja. I felt it was making me high. I asked myself why I had to come so far to find him. What was there between us? What did he mean to me? Nothing! Yet I couldn't let him go. I sat on the bare floor. I told him I didn't think he would recognize me. He too said he didn't expect to see me here. He pulled out a matchbox nestled in his lungi, and lit the kerosene stove. He washed a handful of rice, poured some water into a pot and waited for the flames to turn blue. The fire blazed red, then yellow and finally became blue. Then he placed the pot on the stove and began to talk slowly, like how water takes its time to boil over.

'The river is nothing like the lake. Its current is quite wild. There will always be something floating on it, come summer or monsoon, mostly tree trunks, coconuts, sometimes even animals. You can't blame the river for the current. It's the humans who ought to be blamed. They cut down all the trees on the mountains, let the soil go loose. Some rivers have dried up and some others have become little gorges. Yet man is not done with them. He will dig out the sand; encroach upon the shorelines. Hmm . . . It may seem like nothing more than water, but when pushed to the brink, it can destroy everything!'

I was getting impatient.

'Das . . .'

'Yu–Das . . .' he corrected me.

The pot was warming up. He sat motionless, watching the steam. Suddenly, I was mad at him. I moved beside him and leaned on his shoulders. His moustache and beard glowed blue in the light from the stove. I yearned for a hug from him. But he didn't move. He didn't even look at me.

'I waited for you all these years.'

My voice was morose.

'Why?' he asked. He sounded like he was frozen, deep inside the water, and that his form was now dissolving. My anger got the better of me. 'Das?' I yelled. 'You couldn't read my mind? I need you to love me. I want to live with you.'

'For what?' he mumbled like a fool.

I didn't have an answer. He did have a point. What did I love him for? What was it that I wanted when I live with him? An orphan who dives to recover dead bodies with no more than a nickname: 'Croc'! Why in the world would any woman, young and full of life like me, even fall for a man who reeks of the stink from the dead? I leaned further on his chest languidly. He continued to stare at the stove, faking a smile. I was going crazy in my torment and despair. I told him things that even I wasn't paying attention to: 'Listen! Don't you remember the afternoon that day? We spoke about a lot of things and we were soaking wet. Have you forgotten that you taught boys about girls? Didn't I kiss you? Didn't you have feelings when I touched you? Tell me the truth, Das. Aren't you aroused by the woman in me?'

He didn't answer any of my questions. He remained silent and motionless. Only the water kept boiling above the blue flames with yellow petals.

He lay down on the makeshift bed made of logwood. When the rice was cooked, I turned off the stove and sat beside him. Darkness and silence that smelled of kerosene filled the room. I dearly wished my life would end at that moment. I couldn't think of a reason to go on living if he were to reject me. I cried soundlessly. The river flowed tenderly lest a stone be thrown in to stir up a splash. I hadn't noticed when he slipped his arms that had refused to open up, around my shoulders and begun to caress me. He held me close to his chest and afterwards spoke in a fragile incantation:

'We were all young. It was a terrible time. Realizing humankind's capacity for malice, greed and cruelty troubled our conscience. But turning a blind eye to all that would've been a bigger sin. That is what set me off on this path. I was in an undergraduate college. I had great pride in who I was, and that is what they crushed. The kind of pride that every individual should've had wrapped up in his ribcage. When it was smashed to pieces, I lost myself . . . I ended up being nothing more than a traitor.'

Warm tears streamed along his cheeks. My own drenched his chest. A hum emanated from his chest as though reverberating from underneath a massive rock. I imagined he contained an expansive reservoir of tears in his gentle chest.

He continued, 'The most vivid memory of that time will always be a certain room that was darkened, its windows padded with cardboard rags. It stank horribly the moment I walked in. Was it pee, shit, blood or death? People screamed dreadfully all the time. Their ear-splitting howls would break your heart. You knew right away that they had lost their sense of being human. I wished they would die rather than reel in their never-ending traumas. They were my loved ones. It cut me deep to see them tortured. I gave up names without even realizing I had done that. One after another they named somebody else. The captors linked everyone like rings in a chain. They connected the rest to build a story in which I was the only one chosen to be Judas.'

I raised my hands to wipe his tears.

'You are not a Judas.'

K.R. Meera

'I told them, Prema . . . I couldn't possibly . . . I told them what I knew.' He sobbed inconsolably.

'I gave up Sunanda. I was in love with her. Yet I told them her name. She was way bolder than I ever was. It didn't matter how much they tortured her, she wouldn't cry. I ratted on another comrade when I couldn't bear to watch her suffer any more. They killed Sunanda and Rajan, a friend of hers. It was I who threw their bodies in the gorge. I could never sleep, Prema. I can sink into a lake, plunge into an ocean or float away upon any river, but the roar from that ravine will still hum in my ears. I am a traitor. I really was betraying myself.'

His chest heaved with the beat of his own cries. My head was spinning. I lost my mooring in the agony of the moment and I drowned in the depths of pain and delirium. He wept all night.

'You've got to sleep,' I whispered in torpor.

'I can't sleep, Prema,' he said hugging me tightly. 'You don't know. A traitor can never sleep.'

He must not have slept that night. I, however, slumbered soundly with the reassuring thought that I was loved. In my sleep, I dreamed of red creepers with giant leaves in murky light. I walked across two craggy mountains on a hanging bridge which was withering from the far end. The bridge collapsed halfway through my walk. It descended into the abyss in the shape of a kingfisher and I was a pearl fish bouncing out of the bird's beak. Falling through the air was the same as sinking in water. In my frenzy of love, both seemed alike. My only concern was whose cadaver it would be, waiting at the bottom with a chuckle in its open eyes!

Even in my dream I was envious of the girl, Sunanda. Yudas would be mine. I needed him. I'd lead him into a new life when he woke up. Together we'd fight for a new world. A brave new world. New power for people. 'Long Live the Revolution,' I whispered. 'Strength to the Naxalbari.'

When I woke up in the morning Yudas wasn't home. The cold rice was kept uncovered on the stove, forsaken by even the crows believed to be our forefathers. Only the dampness of our mingled tears remained in my chest. The new world we aspired to seemed empty and doomed. I returned to the hostel feeling hollow, like a dead body that had surfaced on the water on the third day.

FOUR

'She was murdered. I know she was! Amma took her last breath bawling her lungs out. Ugh! Why in the world should one cry? I was bedridden having delivered a baby. This house used to be a leafy shack. The police walked all over us. They beat the shit out of my husband. He became a TB patient, couldn't do a thing. He was hurting like hell until he died. Don't think I say this only because she was my younger sister! She was some woman, well-built and healthy, had a mind strong enough to beat even the menfolk. She knew all along that it would end up like it did. She'd say, "What if a few of us were to go? Let the rest of you live your life in peace?" In the end she was gone, just like she said she would. What about the rest? Did their lives get any better? I don't know, child. Sometimes I think they did. Don't you think their sacrifice ought to be the reason why folks like us are still around eking out a life?'

Sunanda's sister talked while she meshed coconut leaves together. I was trying hard not to see the vision of Sunanda sinking into the gorge.

It took some trouble to find Sunanda's sister. To locate her I pretended to be a journalist working on a story on the Emergency. The grey-haired retired schoolmaster whom I got acquainted with at the extreme leftist CPI-ML office laughed sarcastically. 'Nothing kills me more than these features in print! The torturers, Padikkal, Pulikkodan et al pale in comparison to the fantasy literature peddled by your ilk.' I smiled, feeling guilty. He didn't realize that the reason behind my smile was my love for Yudas. He knew very little about Sunanda. 'The only evidence of Sunanda and Rajan's arrests had been Das's words.' After my father, he was the second person to call Yudas by that name. My heart skipped a beat.

'Das?' I asked as though I'd never heard of him.

'Yes, Das. You've never heard of him, have you? Oh! Weren't there many more people like Rajan and Das in those days? This is J.U. Das. A wise guy. He is still around somewhere, but I don't know where. His heart must be broken.'

'Did he love Sunanda?' I asked him, concealing my envy.

'Oh! One heard many such tales. Didn't all that happen in a different period, child? It was hardly a time for infatuation. Folks had begun to sacrifice their lives for bigger causes. What should've been given more importance was the fact that so many youngsters from all corners of the state had swept up to resist the government rather than this harping on the torture saga.' He sighed.

Sunanda's sister sighed exactly the same way.

'There were a lot of them. Many people like you came to me looking for old stories. How was she tortured? Who bashed whom? When did I last see her? . . . Isn't that all over? Whoever is gone is gone. Das told me she was thrown into the gorge. It must be true. They caned her legs black and blue. Poured chilli powder all over the gashes. Pummelled her chest to a pulp. Her nipples were crushed and fell off. She wouldn't cry though. She took after our father. He was like her. He too was thrashed at the toddy labour union march. Blood gushed out of his mouth, yet he chanted "Inquilab Zindabad".'

I was tearing up. My face drooped and I sobbed. That was for the sake of my father.

Unaware of that, she offered me solace. 'Don't cry child. It happened a while ago. It's done. Buck up.'

She continued, 'Sunanda finished the tenth standard and attended a typewriting school. She dreamed of passing the public service exams and securing a job. I raised her. She wasn't just a younger sister, but more like a daughter to me. I never so much as pinched her. She got in touch with the group at the library. Arrests had already begun. Some came out of prison too. Nothing would turn Sunanda away from the group. Who knows how those God-awful murderers hurt her? Das said her sari was stripped off her. She was made to stand up naked. Beaten. When they bashed her hind legs, chunks of flesh flew all over the place. Even that didn't make her cry. She was like that. She'd never cry. Das told me that they couldn't get anything out of her.'

'Das . . . Did you see Das after that?'

'Yes. He comes here once in a while. Who else has he got but some of us?'

'Were they in love?'

She smiled.

'She was beautiful. And above all, she had a steely inner strength. Das adored her. Was it love? Or affection? I don't know. He believes she was caught and murdered because of him. It couldn't be. They would have got her even if he hadn't. The time was such, wasn't it?'

'Didn't Das betray Sunanda and Rajan?'

'Huh! What did he even know? Nothing! But he convinced himself that that was what happened . . .

'Das was a kind boy. A poet. He loved Sunanda. He loved everyone. He came from a decent family. All he had was his mother. She died seeing her only son's life in ruins.'

'Where is Das now?' I inquired.

'Who knows? He comes here once in a while. Gives me some money, even though I don't need any. But he will feel bad if I tell him that, so I take it.'

Sunanda's elder sister's daughter walked into the house when I was about to leave. She had been doing a course at the Amrita Institute. 'Sunanda looked just like her,' said the elder sister. I looked at the girl with wide eyes. She had a dark complexion, and a fine face which radiated a kind of resolve. I suddenly felt inferior. Das, who had known a girl like Sunanda, could never love someone like me—a hollow woman, the kind who would never sink and was burdened with a reprehensible legacy including attempts to cover up the stench of rotten flesh by burning incense.

I bought myself a copy of the Bible for the first time when I took leave of Sunanda's sister. I browsed through it, trying to find sections referring to Judas. I read about Judas from the chapter titled 'Apostles' Creed':

Men and brethren, this scripture must needs have been fulfilled, which the Holy Ghost by the mouth of David spake before concerning Judas, which was guide to them that took Jesus. For he was numbered with us, and had obtained part of this ministry. Now this man purchased a field with the reward of iniquity; and falling headlong, he burst asunder in the midst, and all his bowels gushed out. And it was known unto all the dwellers at Jerusalem; insomuch as that field is called in their proper tongue, Aceldama, that is to say, the field of blood.

I put the book down. I tried to forget Yudas in each of the following nights. I reeled under a bout of severe depression. I became habituated with headaches and the loss of appetite. Ulcers and sinusitis made me miserable. I saw my father in uniform when I closed my eyes. In a dark hall where sunlight was kept out with raggedy sheets of paper on the windows, my father lined up wiry young men whose bosoms swelled with pride. He drank standing at the bottom of a giant pile of bottles. My mouth tasted the salt-and-sour blood which my father ruthlessly beat out of the youngsters. I suffered an unbearable pain as though a nipple was ripped right out of my breast.

I didn't have enough money to support a lengthy medical recovery. So I went back home, unable to complete the diploma course in that town. I remember the day I returned to the village on the shores of the lake. I had taken a commuter bus. By the time I got down at the foot of a banyan tree surrounded by a ring of dry leaves fluttering in the breeze from the lake, I was tired and couldn't move an inch. My wilted, moth-infested feudal home waited for me. Cirrhosis and tremors had already left my father bedridden for the rest of his life. My father's elder sister, Balu's mother, remained the only one to take care of him. The main source of our income was the bank interest she earned on the insurance money she received when her husband passed away. I tried hard not to think of Balu when she served food on my plate with an empty look in her sunken eyes. Every time I remembered him, the image of his coral-shaped face with innumerable holes came to my mind. I inquired jokingly if people weren't drowning in the lake any more. My aunt had a scowl on her face. I have had only corpses to remember, their ghastly dead faces, nibbled at by fishes, that became pale and swollen underwater.

Sometimes I would walk to the south end of our backyard and watch the lake in the distance from under the expansive old mango tree. The lake lay wearily among the hills like a beached whale. The lush green had vanished from the slopes. The tall rubber trees beyond the faraway mound had been cleared to make way for new plantations, leaving the mound barren. A couple of barges floated by lazily sometime in the day. And I remembered him even when I didn't want to. 'Croc' Yudas. He kept going deeper into the abyss of my mind, hauling the dead bodies he recovered on to the shore of my memory.

I spent many years at home. The house had turned into a torture camp for me. My young brothers had already become grown-ups. One joined the Pentecostal group and the other became a bootlegger and a notorious criminal in the community. I stayed in a room where a garlanded black-and-white portrait of my mother hung. I was never loved by my mother. She never had been loved by my father. None of us has ever had anyone else's love. Life had always unfolded under an emergency of some kind. Nobody dared to open up. Nor did they dare to love. The police arrested my brother on the day my ulcer got worse and blood began to seep into my mouth. My father lay on the bed, unable to lift his head. A police van arrived in the middle of the night. As soon as my aunt opened the door, our courtyard reverberated with the sound of police boots. I came out with bleary eyes only to be thrust aside as they hollered, 'BLOODY ROTTEN BITCH OF AN ASS-IMPALER!' I fell on to the doorsteps opening into my father's room. My forehead slashed open after it slammed into the wall, and blood gushed out. At the same time, blood from the ulcer oozed out of my mouth. I felt elated in that moment to be able to spill some blood for my father's band of brothers. After the police took my brother away, my father sat on the bed in disquiet. The next day I was asked to visit the police station, only to be informed that he had escaped from lock-up soon after he was arrested. My brother might have died in custody. His dead body emerged from the lake the day after.

The fishermen didn't want to pull my brother's body out of the water. Naturally I thought of Yudas. In my younger days he would spread his arms like a fishing net over the lake before he leapt into it. The lake submitted herself to him like a languorous lover, unfolding the secrets of her womb for him. This time it was a Tamil who came to recover the corpse. The dark, stocky man had yellow eyes. He was drunk before he waded into the lake. I didn't have tears in my eyes when I watched my brother's corpse brought to the shore. The corpse had blue streaks on its thighs, chest and back. No sooner had the body been laid down than the Tamil man began to haggle. A thousand and five hundred, he demanded. Some in the crowd bickered. I didn't have any money on me, so the villagers set up a collection to pay him. My brother's body was stiff and bent inwards even before he was pulled out of the water. Those who were arrested along with my brother said he died when he was put under the rollers during torture. Yet I couldn't bring myself to cry. His body too was laid in the front yard of the house and surrounded by burning incense sticks. Some people carried my father out to show him the body.

'My son . . . my son,' Father whimpered a little.

'The police killed him with the roller rods,' I said aloud for everyone to hear.

'The police?'

There was a look of distrust in Father's tired and crevassed eyes. I relished that look. I suddenly felt an affection for my brother. He had paid the dues for our father with his life. Our house sank back into the gloom. The scent of incense deprived me of sleep again. I tossed and turned in bed thinking of Yudas. I couldn't continue to live without his love. It's not just the traitor; his lover too can't have sleep. Her body too never ceases to feel like it is being scorched. I was terrified at the thought of my life being eaten away by termites inside this dilapidated and rancid Naalukettu. I wasn't going to let that happen. I would run to the lake, tie a stone to my legs and throw myself to the deep end of the water. My body would undulate in the waves at the bottom, rooted into the crimson dirt like a leafless water plant. I imagined Yudas closing in to recover my corpse. I wanted to cry. I would allow only Yudas to make me cry.

FIVE

'Lord, you know everyone's heart. Show us which of these two you have chosen to take over this apostolic ministry, which Judas left to go where he belongs.' Then they cast lots, and the lot fell to Matthias; so he was added to the eleven apostles.

I read this section from the Bible every day and each time I thought about Yudas. My love for him was a burning flame in my heart that refused to be put out. My heart melted like a candle so that the flame could stay alive. I cried for him, and in my mind I trudged the path to Kakkayam camp every day to submit to the lashings in his stead. My illness only got worse with time. The room where my father lay was enveloped in a rotten stench.

I would see his emaciated form wrapped in black wool, and I would shudder the same way I had when I saw the corpse in the deep end of the lake where I sank for the first time. He couldn't sleep. Some nights he would randomly repeat in his frail voice. 'Who is crying . . .? Water rumbles!' At other times he would jabber, 'Water in the gorge.' I didn't ask him which gorge it was. He too had long fallen into the gorge's depths. Once in a while he bawled as though his heart had just been broken. Sometimes he spoke incessantly. He must be opening himself up, I would think. Tormented by his memories, Father too might be ratting himself out.

There was no word on Yudas. I wrote to Sunanda's sister sometimes. She would reply through postcards. Yudas had moved to Malampuzha, she wrote once. She didn't say what he did there.

He was here last Sunday. He gave me five hundred rupees. I asked him about you. But he walked away saying nothing, didn't even touch the black tea . . .

My tears fell on the shapely letters on her postcard. Malampuzha. I chanted the word in my dreams and in my waking hours. Perhaps he is able to find many dead bodies there. I envied the dead bodies. I felt vengeful towards Yudas again. With a melting heart I explored opportunities to go to Malampuzha. I traded blood in a clinic across the lake to meet travel expenses. There wasn't much blood in my body; I squeezed out whatever I had. That night I boarded a Palakkad-bound train, having lied about my need to visit the college in Kozhikode to receive a certificate.

At dawn I was sitting in a bus, leather bag in hand, feeling the moist air rushing through the window, and anxiously wondering how I was going to find Yudas. I got down near the Malampuzha dam and strolled along the road aimlessly. I walked past the ropeway and a coffee shop behind a cotton tree in full bloom to reach a little bridge leading to the guest house. Under the bridge was the lake and on its brink stood three policemen while a few other bystanders huddled under a tall coral tree. I hoped someone had died by drowning for it meant Yudas would certainly be there. I really wanted someone to die. I carefully manoeuvred my way around the rocky ledges to get near the shore. It was a homicide brought on by gangster violence. The corpse had been thrown into the dam. Regrettably, by the time I arrived the body had already been recovered. I glanced despairingly at the dead body, covered haphazardly with a white sheet which was sodden. The pebbles under it were drenched too. The corpse's face was partially turned towards the side as though it had begun to look around for someone. Perhaps he was stabbed in the back by a close friend—a backstabber! We all might take a last look at a traitor in exactly the same way. I stood there, watching the cadaver's hair flutter in the breeze.

A boat rattled towards the ferry. After all the tourists disembarked, the dead body was transferred on to the boat. Following the jostling crowd, I was the last passenger to step in. I chatted up the policeman who sat on the steps at the entrance of the boat. I introduced myself and mentioned my father's name during the conversation. He told me Yudas's whereabouts.

This time Yudas had built himself a leafy shack that almost touched the water if you stretched your legs far enough. He had a lit beedi between his lips while frying a fish impaled on a rod. I stood outside glumly, unable to enter the shack since the state of my health wouldn't let me bend. He saw my feet from inside. The beedi slipped out of his mouth and lay fuming on the plain dirt as he got up with a start, crawled out through the tiny door and stared at me. He had trouble getting his breath back. Sighing slowly as though he'd resigned to the fact that he had been found, he called me in. I didn't look at him, nor did I move an inch. The waves from the departed boat beat against the rock that rose in the middle of the reservoir, its concentric rings exposed by the ebbing water. A large eagle sat listlessly atop a golden shower tree in the middle of the islet. The waves caressed my feet.

'I've been expecting you here, Prema.'

He sounded cold. Again he invited me inside. I broke into tears. That wasn't the welcome I'd anticipated. A cruel lover. I looked at him reproachfully. He smiled like an imbecile. In the end I gave up. With great effort, I bent and entered through the door. Inside, underneath the roof of coconut leaves which had been thatched together and was held aloft by the mesh of bamboo props that served as walls, there was hardly enough space for the two of us to lie down on our backs. I felt like I was lying on top of a thin layer of dirt below which the lake billowed—the water was that close to me; the floor was muddy and moist.

'I have been expecting you,' he repeated. The fish being cooked in the sputtering oil turned a golden brown. I glared at him now.

'I knew you would come,' he said. 'You would come. You'd keep looking for me everywhere. And you would remind me of bygone stuff. I knew that,' he said coldly. I felt a mad rush inside me but when I looked at him, the flow of rage slowed all of a sudden and I became tender again. I quietly watched the fish. He too was quiet. He got up when the evening darkened.

'Where are you going?' I inquired resentfully.

He laughed like a fool. 'You will find me no matter where I go. Won't you?' he said it again as though he had reconciled to the prospect of my scouting for him.

'I will!' I said mock-threateningly.

He'd lost again. My breasts ached as though their nipples were ripped out. I felt weak every time I looked at his face. He was my Naxalite. He carried the burden of human sins to redeem this world.

'I am ill, Das,' I whispered through tears.

'Yu-Das,' he corrected.

After a pause, he asked, 'Why did you go looking for Sunanda's sister?'

I didn't respond.

'You are nothing like Sunanda!' Yudas blew up suddenly. 'I can never forget her, Prema. I close my eyes and I see the gorge. I see her body sinking into the water. You haven't seen that river, have you? The water has a slimy green tinge. Its current is like an immensely wild force of nature. You cannot swim in there. Throw a stone and the current will bounce it around until it begs to drown. But you should've seen how Sunanda sank into it. I am haunted by that vision all the time. A quick fall. She went right through.

'I was at the far end of a rocky ledge, overlooking the gorge. They asked me to toss her out. I'd become too weak from puking blood. Blood is man's modesty, Prema. When he is made to throw it up, he falls apart. I bent as far as I could when I flung her away. I wanted to go along with her. But they had tied a rope around my waist and secured the other end to a tree. I must be the world's most despicable lover. Man becomes a beast the moment he has chains around his waist or feet. What man needs is freedom. Not only to run or walk, but to think, dream and die too. The waves couldn't conquer her. Instead she conquered the waves. Oh! What strength she possessed. It isn't the might of the body, but the power of the mind. I have never seen a woman like that. She never lost to either water or blood. She just never did.'

Tears brimmed my eyes. My heart writhed and scalded as if it had fallen into boiling oil in a frying pan. I wished to burn away completely.

'Sunanda is dead.' I reminded him sadistically. 'Who's to gain if you keep talking about her? She, who is long dead? Or you, who are still alive? What about me? What about the world?'

Yudas lost steam instantly.

'Prema, don't. Let's talk something else.'

I got angrier.

'No! Let's talk more about Sunanda. Who was Sunanda? A girl. She joined the group by accident. She was nothing like me. Granted. I was born in a feudal home and grew up there. Yet I believed in you and your ideology. Finding you was never a question of choice. I waited for you alone. I wanted only *you*. My love should mean more to you than Sunanda's.'

I was shaking with anger and grief.

'Sunanda never loved you at all. I will tell you whom she loved. Rajan! That is the reason she ended her life right next to him in the gorge.'

'Stop!'

Yudas lunged at my throat. As he tightened his hands around my neck, my eyes bulged and tongue protruded from my mouth. My mouth and nose began to bleed immediately. He let go of me.

'What happened now?' I asked, struggling to breathe. 'Kill me if you dare. And then throw me in the ravine.'

Yudas retreated. He sat quietly like a convict for a while, as if he had been drained of all his energy. I rubbed my neck gently to regain my voice. My eyes were wet. My voice cracked as I spoke without a hint of ire.

'On the third day you will have to dive in and pull me out of the water. That will be my greatest wish come true.'

My love for him cut through my garbled voice. He must have recognized it, for he too was looking more than exhausted. It's not just blood that is private to a man; love is another secret he wouldn't want to part with. He'd be weary of throwing up that too. Yudas lay on his back on the mud floor. Tiny specks of dirt got stuck on his body in random places. I didn't move an inch from where I'd been sitting. But I extended my arm to gently caress his silky hair. The fish was completely fried in the boiling oil by now. I turned off the stove. Darkness enveloped the shack. I continued to caress his hair.

After a long time, when my fingers began to tire, he spoke again.

'It doesn't matter who wins or loses, Prema. It is more important to make sense and resist. We were weak. We fantasized about becoming a band of potent force, a bunch of young things, who had no clue what life really was! We were passionate, honest and pure at heart. That's all we were. We took up arms. Our goal was to rid this world of injustice. We longed for a fertile earth, clean air and pure water. It was a difficult period. The lure of wealth and a life of luxury had begun to entice people. Charmed by the colour of money, the representatives of people, who had grown up in poverty themselves, forgot everything. They wrote off our land to money launderers and black marketeers. Someone had to challenge them, but in reality there was nobody. Everyone was afraid of the machinery of the state. If only we'd won then.'

He was out of breath.

'All state machines have the same face, Das,' I whispered. 'Power will corrupt you too.'

'If we'd won, I wouldn't have lost Sunanda,' he whimpered.

I was mad at him again.

'You are insane. You know nothing about this world or life. A fool, that's who you are. I who've loved you must be a bigger fool!'

I tried to get up but then settled down again.

He peered at me for a while. Then he got up and walked out, towards the reservoir. Through a tiny crack in the hut I could see moonlight fall across the sky. Beneath the glint, he swam soundlessly. When he came back, he brought a bucketful of water for me. 'I will fix a cover for you behind the hut. Please wash yourself,' he said.

His words warmed my body. He does remember that I do have a body to wash. I regretted that it had been weakened by disease and destitution. It craved for him. When I returned to the hut, wrapped in the scent of Lifebuoy soap, he served me rice on a couple of dry teak leaves. The fried fish was placed on top of the rice.

'I don't want the fish,' I said.

'Huh?'

'I don't want it,' I repeated.

Fish reminded me of dead bodies. There are dead people at the bottom of every waterbody.

If you venture deep into the water, towards the bottom, you will find fish slithering out of every corpse. He fed me balls of plain rice which he rolled in his hands. I ate hungrily. Tears streamed down as I chewed. His silhouette in the darkened hut resembled a hermit. He got rid of the leaves outside, washed his hands and came back in, pulling down a leaf door behind him. He spread a mat on the floor. When I stood there incomprehensibly, he approached me and held my shoulder to lead me to the mat. Moonlight beamed brighter in the sky. I hoped he would accept me as a woman tonight. I wanted to push the leaf door open and lie on his chest while I marvelled at the moon. I leant on his chest. He kept caressing my shoulders and hair. His fingers had become soft having been in the water for ages. By the time he moved his fingers across my head, I was sleepy.

'Where are you going to run away next?' I fought sleep as I inquired. My voice was damp with love and grief.

'Das, do you love me?'

Yudas didn't respond. Instead he continued stroking the strands of my hair. I yearned to hear him say that he loved me. He didn't. I despaired that he would never say those words. I hugged him tightly. His body warmed up in my embrace. The brimming reservoir outside muffled its sobs. I closed my eyes slowly. These fingers belong to a revolutionary, I thought proudly. They were caressing me to sleep. I felt the waves sway under the mat. I was slumbering in his lap atop a carpet of water. I was living a dream. I slept deep that night.

I woke up in the morning to find that there was no one around. What remained were my little leather bag, the soiled cloth I had shed yesterday, me and my virginity. Meanwhile, he, his reddish-dirt-stained clothes, kerosene stove and vessels were gone. Even the mat on which I had slept had vanished into thin air. I sat in shock like a poor little girl who'd slept in a magician's mansion. The palace had turned into a thorny jungle. He had duped me again; thrown me alive into a gorge.

How long would I have to wait till I met him again? Where could I look? And yet he would fool me again. I would allow only him to fool me.

SIX

My Lord and the Highest Honourable
Parameswaran Sir,

This letter is written by Vasudevan who
was fortunate enough to be in the service at
Kakkayam camp under your benevolence.
I trust that you remember my voluntary
retirement from the service. I am respectfully
writing this letter to you with liberty and in
fond memory of being the beneficiary of your
kind affection while I was in the service. After
retirement my life has fallen into hard times.
Ill health has laid me down. My financial
situation is miserable. The carrier of this letter
is my daughter. She is getting on in age. It is my
wish that she find a husband from the service.
Would there be someone in your memory or
circle kind enough to marry the daughter of

a poor policeman? Save for this run-down Naalukettu, I have no other means or gold to offer. I conclude this letter with the belief and expectation that you will understand the plight of an old colleague and do what can be done.

May you be showered with good health and long life!

Humbly and in obedience,

Vasudevan

I reread the letter my father handed to me. Suddenly, I wanted to throw up blood. Parameswaran was the notorious supervising police officer who was nicknamed 'Beast'. When I had agreed to meet my father's superior officer, I had never imagined *this* was the purpose of the visit.

I'd found work as a teacher in a computer institute that had opened recently in the village. I disliked teaching. But a salary of a thousand rupees was too good to pass up. It did help to buy medicines for my father, aunt and myself. The odour of the medicines lingered in the central courtyard of our feudal house. The pillars that supported the house and the courtyard of our crumbling grand old home had wilted. The little vanity mirror I used sometime in my teenage years on an eroded iron bar had become blanched. I rarely used the mirror now. Every time I looked into it I saw Balu's face peeking from behind. He was growing a moustache when he died. Its growth halted midway and was distinctly visible on Balu's face in the mirror.

I was travelling out of the village after a long time. There was no news about Yudas any more. Postcards from Sunanda's sister had also tapered off. I had agreed to carry the letter only because I wanted to use this opportunity to visit her. I hated the 'Beast' from my gut. He was responsible for making Yudas spit blood. The only redeeming thing about him was that when there were inquiries on the many deaths in police custody, he took complete blame and punishment for the dead victims of iron-rod-roll-up tortures under his watch, and shielded the subordinates who'd worked for him.

It was an old-fashioned two-storey building. The house appeared lifeless, having not been painted for ages. I shuddered to think that I was about to meet the man who had once run the biggest killing machine in the history of this land. The door was ajar. I pressed the bell, and a quivering voice answered, asking me to come in. I kept the leather bag on the porch, tugged at the end of my sari and walked towards the entrance. The house's interior was dimly lit. The Beast was reading the Bhagavadgita, sitting on a doormat on the floor. When he asked who it was one more time, I stepped inside.

I said, 'I am Prema, daughter of Vasudevan, a police constable from the old time.'

He seemed to recall the name from his memory. He got up. I looked at the old man in front of me inquisitively. There was no indication of beastliness on his face. A lonely man in his old age who appeared to have nobody to rub balm on his aching back or serve him a glass of water should he get thirsty. His face was pale, having been indoors for a long time. Greyed stubble had replaced the handlebar moustache. The only thing that indicated this old man used to be a cop was his probing stare as he looked at me closely with aged pupils from beneath white eyebrows.

'I don't see old colleagues. I am not in touch with any of them. What brings you here?'

The Beast spoke in a gentle voice that made one believe that he never had to yell at anything. I remembered compassionately my father's hyperbole describing how the Beast's bellowing during the torture sessions had caused tremors in Konippaara hill, bringing rocks tumbling to its base. No towering mountain of authority had survived for my father to perch himself upon. There were no more rocks fragile enough to fall off even if someone roared his lungs out.

'If you need me to do something, it's not going to happen,' he warned. 'I am not capable of being useful for anything now. Vasudevan should be able to figure that much by himself.'

'I haven't come out of any particular need,' I replied quickly. 'My father has the greatest respect for you. He is worried because he hasn't heard from you in a long time. I'd come to this place for another purpose and I thought my visit would give him some comfort.'

The Beast's face lit up a bit. He expressed his happiness at being visited after a long time by someone who was not a reporter or a news features writer from the press. He went back inside and returned with a cup of coffee. The Beast was all alone in the house. In the visitor's room there was a garlanded picture of an elderly lady who appeared to be his wife. It was a black-and-white picture similar to my mother's. There were other photos below it.

'She was my wife,' the Beast said. 'Passed away . . . in an accident,' he added wiping his tears as he gazed at the framed photo.

'Children?'

The Beast's eyes welled up again.

'All gone . . . Enough said!'

I was curious to find out how they had all gone. How does time's state machinery administer justice to beasts? I blew on the hot coffee to cool it before taking a sip as I looked up on the photos. One of them was a full-figured portrait of an extravagantly bejewelled woman who resembled the Beast. He informed me that she was murdered. 'Her marriage was a mistake. The boy was mentally ill. I lost my senses when I was told about his family, privileges, position and career. It was a huge mistake. He put her in a suitcase after cutting her into . . .' The Beast couldn't finish his sentence.

'The other daughter had cancer. She lived with a big hole in her cheek, causing great grief to all of us. The third daughter committed suicide. Her husband had an affair. She took poison on the day she was to get divorced.'

I listened to him as I sipped the coffee. He made really good coffee. The Beast must have had a gift for cooking. Ever since I had fallen in love with Yudas, sob stories had ceased to affect me. Who has more woes than he? What blade is sharper than our separation? Who is afraid of rivulets and pools when one is already mired far below the muddy layers at the bottom of a lake?

'Have you had a chance to meet any of the Naxalites?' I asked casually. What I needed to know was if anyone had ever come back to avenge the Beast. He, however, let out a sigh of relief.

'Only once. One person. He was the one who pulled out the body of my boy when he drowned.'

The coffee cup slid out of my hands and shattered into a hundred pieces. I stood there stunned.

'It's okay,' the Beast said. 'Wash the coffee off of your sari, kid. I will clean this up.'

My limbs wouldn't move. My heart stopped for a while. I could just ask: Who recovered the body? But my hands and legs began to shake as I thought about it. I imagined Yudas hauling out the Beast's son's body just like he had pulled out Balu's corpse from the bottom of the lake. I couldn't help but holler, 'Oh, God!' in the face of time's machinery of state. When I returned after cleaning my sari, the Beast was scooping up the broken pieces of the cup with a little broom. I insisted that he give me the broom and let me clean the floor. I raked in a sharp piece and it cut my finger.

'I see blood, kid!' the Beast cried out. That shocked me more. It was incredible to watch a former cop who had made history by causing an extraordinary number of young boys to throw up blood now go berserk at the sight of a few drops of blood.

'Blood,' I repeated after him. 'When did you begin to fear blood, sir?'

The Beast was taken aback. Then he smiled gently. 'It was youth, kid. You wouldn't be scared to shed blood when you are young. It's different when you become old.' The Beast spread out his wrinkly palms with loose wobbly skin. 'It's been a while since these hands have had blood on them.'

'Do you feel remorseful?' I asked eagerly.

'For what?' he groaned. 'The state is a big machine, kid. A policeman is no more than a bolt or a nut in it. We couldn't have done anything by ourselves. We were just tools. Tools at the state's disposal. Each one of us was like that. Only the state mattered. *It* had to stay. Didn't God, Lord Krishna himself, say the same in the Bhagavadgita? I used to believe that my children died to atone for my crimes. Most of my colleagues' families were torn apart. Some became gravely ill. The children of a few have gone astray. Others have lost their homes. Were these nothing more than the consequences of a collective curse from the youngsters whom we brutalized till they threw up gore? I don't know. We didn't think like that. I was doing my duty.'

'But there were too many of them. The young men who'd gone under . . .' I asked despondently as I listened to the Beast.

'Have no doubt, they were dangerous,' the Beast cackled. 'Unbridled minds. Brash adolescence. Hot blood. How in the world were they going to know the good from bad at that age? Their stupid actions were more than just trouble. We had no choice but to beat some sense into them. It had to be done for the state. I was a different person then. My philosophy of that time was different. Time, kid, time was the sole reason for everything. Those young men and us, we were just tools in time's box.' The Beast leaned back in his reclining chair with a deep sigh, and began fanning himself with a towel tucked over his shoulders. He did look like a pale skinny harmless man of faith.

'The rebel who recovered your drowned son, did you know him?'

The Beast slanted his head to look at me.

'Hmm. I couldn't recall him at the beginning. He yelled "Naxalbari Zindabad" at me, throwing his arms up with a folded fist. He kicked my boy's body and challenged me: "Arrest me if you dare." I recognized him right away. His name was Das, an innocent lad!'

My heart began to pound. It throbbed out of pride and anguish brought on by my thoughts of Yudas.

'Then, what happened then?' I asked anxiously. I felt disappointed not to have been there to see it. My Yudas. The moment when he was exacting his greatest revenge. When was it? How did it happen?

'I heard from my father,' I said, 'that all the secrets were beaten out of a man called Das. And he was made to toss a couple of bodies into the ravine.'

I was fishing for the Beast's story.

He glared at me probingly. 'What is it that you really want to know?'

The Beast now bared the eyes of a cop from old times, making me panic. Then, abruptly, he sighed again. 'Das was a skinny boy. But he had a steely mind. He didn't look it, but he got cheeky when we began the treatment. His and my ages were such. I was there for the state. The state couldn't bow to a criminal, could it? I got mad. I was on my feet for nearly twenty-four hours, skipping breaks even for the loo, so that I could beat him into submission. I tried the belt first, then the baton and then the roller. It was a lot of labour for both the tormenter and the subject. But he never uttered a word. Finally, it became a matter of pride. I poured liquor into him. Water-boarded him. Scalded his body. Shoved food into his throat and made him throw it all up immediately after. Twisted his balls with a wrench. Poked his anus . . .'

By now I was shaking. Puzzled, the Beast trained his inquisitive stare at me. I was sweating profusely.

'Do you know him?' he asked, in a voice that was becoming hoarse.

I was worried that he might interrogate me despite his long break.

'I know everyone,' I said, trying to force a smile. 'I have been listening to all these stories since I was five.'

'Oh! I thought—' The Beast fanned himself again.

'Wasn't there a woman? I heard her name was Sunanda?' I tried to sound as guileless as I possibly could.

The Beast laughed. 'Yes, she was a good girl.'

I asked him if Das was the one to betray her.

The Beast laughed again: 'There is that moment, kid, when even the most resolute, strong-willed individual breaks down. At one point Das blurted out a name, Sunanda. That's all we needed. We brought her in. We realized as soon as we arrested her that he was a mere infant compared to her. She was the real deal, the revolutionary. Couldn't she have said a word? Couldn't she have cried at least for the sake of it? We beat her repeatedly, but all that did was tire us out. But Das changed as soon as we began to manhandle the lady. He began to sing like a parrot. He told us everything he knew. Poor chap!' The Beast laughed.

My eyes welled up. The heaviness in my heart choked me. Since my pride wouldn't allow me to bawl, I stood there, trying to pull back myself from the brink of it.

'You people killed her, didn't you?'

'We didn't kill anybody. They all killed themselves.' The Beast's voice turned rough. 'It was war, kid. When you set out for war, what matters is whether you fight or not. It was destiny that decided to declare the war. And it was the same destiny that decided who would win, who would lose and who would survive. What is destroyed is not created by me. What is lost is not earned by me. I wasn't there yesterday. I won't be there tomorrow. The post I'd occupied yesterday has been assumed by another person today. Tomorrow he too will be replaced by somebody else. I don't need to repent, kid. This is the cycle of karma. If I have to start all over again, I might do exactly the same. I was loyal to my job. Showed gratitude to the state for the salary it gave me. I decimated those who dared to defy the state. When I beat them up I put all my heart into it. I was never influenced by tears, blood, pleas or bribes. I was a tool. I am not ashamed of it, but I am disappointed at having been picked as one. Why did God choose to use me for the things I had to do? When my wife and children died, I asked myself this question. Couldn't I be one of those government servants who worked from nine to five to earn a salary, took their family for an occasional movie on a weekend and lead their life in peace? Why did God give me the baton, rollers and pistol instead? Why did *my* hands have to be stained with blood? I don't know. Would anything be different even if I tried? No. Perhaps. Who knows? That must have been my lot. Someone had to do it, so I was chosen. Whatever happened, happened for good. Whatever is going to happen will be happening for good. Whatever is happening is also . . .'

My mouth was filled with the taste of sour coffee and acrid blood. It was hard to believe that an old man with such an amiable face was once a beast feasting on the blood of the youth. That he had made the inmates drink their own urine, pierced needles into their penises and forced batons into the uteruses of young women. Power is a magician's hat. Humans who wear it inevitably transform.

Later, as I walked towards the bus stop, a large car displaying 'Kerala State' on its front board raced down the road, the potholes slowing its progress. A convoy jeep carrying cops followed the car. The cop sitting on the left side of the jeep stared at me for as long as he could. It struck fear in me for some reason. It was a revolting stare, which only a cop was capable of. I felt a horseshoe descend on my chest. The nipples from my breasts were about to be ripped out. People around me seemed to be staggering about with penises impaled with needles or uteruses into which batons were rammed that they couldn't get rid of.

Ill health had confined Sunanda's sister to her bed now. She struggled to get up when she saw me walking in. I made coffee for her. She had no news of Yudas any more. It had been two years since he had shown up. He had sent some money to her last year, but there was no word after that. Dejected, I stood up to leave. She asked me to wait for a bit; she had something to show me. She dragged herself up to the attic with great effort and returned with an old box. Inside was a diary. It had belonged to Sunanda.

Bursting with impatience, I snatched it out of her hand. A passport-sized photo was tucked inside the pocket cover of the diary. I gazed at the photo anxiously. A seventeen-year-old girl with wide eyes stared at me. I decided to confront her stare.

'I won't admit defeat,' those eyes seemed to declare.

I fumed. 'You lost when you died,' I whispered vengefully. 'I am alive. To be alive is the real victory.' I turned the pages, reading the words with smouldering eyes.

There was a quote on the first page:

'*O Liberté, que de crimes on commeten ton nom!*' Madame Roland

Oh Liberty, what crimes are committed in thy name!

There were shorthand notes on the next few pages. I came back to the cover page to ponder on Madame Roland's words for a long time. I read them many times over, then confronted Sunanda's stare one more time.

'Can I have this?' I asked.

'This is the only thing I have left of her,' Sunanda's sister said as she strained to breathe again. 'Or you may keep it? Leave just the photo. I need that. It is my wish to have it enlarged and framed and put up somewhere on the wall. At least I hope to.'

I unglued the photo half-heartedly. I returned home at night in the commuter bus.

As I sat in the bus, I suddenly remembered the letter my father had written to the Beast with a plea to find a husband for me. I pulled it out of my purse and slid it inside Sunanda's diary.

I didn't need a bridegroom or a husband. Yudas is all I needed in my life. I would swim far and deep into the lake until my limbs went numb and sank to the bottom. I would die in the crimson mud from where Yudas would recover me. This was how he would get over the grief of a betrayer. I opened the first page of the diary again. 'Oh, Liberty, what crimes are committed in thy name!'

It took an endless twelve hours to reach home. My fellow passengers dozed off in the bus. I pushed the shutter open. Outside the window, garish street lights ran backwards while I reread the shapely letters from the diary as they clashed to break out beyond the cold blast piercing through the window.

Oh, Liberty!

SEVEN

'I couldn't sleep at night. I'd hear some sound—a footstep, the revving of a motor car's engine, or a bell from a bicycle—and I'd suddenly be on my feet. The thought that they were here for me was terrifying. I'd be on my bed, frozen. Didn't I have those documents with me—the blueprint for the planned action? I wasn't part of the organization, yet when Das asked me to keep it, I agreed. My house was safe; no one would suspect anything. But ever since, to tell you the truth, child, I haven't been able to sleep at night at all. I can only sleep during the day. I know the Emergency has been long gone. Everyone has forgotten all about it. But I am yet to sleep in peace for once. I am worried that those days might be coming back. Maybe with another name . . . Sometimes I think we are already there. We just aren't able to recognize it.'

My mind was ablaze as I walked alongside Surendran *mash* who wore a saffron cloth. He didn't say anything about Yudas. Whenever I brought up Yudas's name, he would go on about the dark days of that period. I was here to attend a wedding. Sunanda's sister's daughter was getting married. I had no doubt that Yudas would come for the ceremony. So I ignored my ailments and uncertainties on the road for a long-distance journey. It had been five years since I met him.

In the meantime I had changed my job twice. Having been on leave for too many days due to my chronic ulcer, my employer at my first job dismissed me. I then took up a biller's job in a shop, but the heat and dust on the premises worsened my condition. After that I became a scribe to a wealthy woman who had writerly aspirations. She lived in a waterfront home near Lake Ashtamudi. Her husband was an affluent industrialist. The job was comfortable. She would recline on a chair facing the lake, from the morning onwards, and discuss the story she had been thinking of writing. There was nothing much in it. She wanted to write a book based on her own life. She believed she had an extraordinary tale to tell. Let's just say even if it had been truly extraordinary, she didn't seem to have the courage to bare it all. Anyway, I got good food and time enough to sleep well in that house. I was lodged in a room in the guest house which overlooked the lake. Visitors and guests walked in and out of my employer's house all the time. I noticed that excess food was thrown in the coconut grove in the yard behind the kitchen where it would rot. Whenever I saw it I would worry about Yudas. Was he getting enough food for himself? Or was he wandering around, high on ganja on an empty stomach? And filling it up with pints of toddy?

Sunanda's sister brought up Yudas in our conversation as soon as we met even though I hadn't asked her about him: 'Did you know? Our Das isn't well. He is bedridden. Please go and see him.' I was dazed to hear the news. Before I could prod her further, it was time to begin the wedding rituals. As the sounds of drums and flutes reverberated and the rites were carried out, I was burning inside, thinking about Yudas. I could imagine him curled up inside a makeshift hut at the edge of a reservoir whose name I didn't know. Where could he be? I inquired after his whereabouts from Sunanda's sister at the first chance I got. Fatigued from the bustle of wedding activities and the persistent heaving to fight her asthma, she looked at me and said, 'Sethu mash must know. He received a letter from Das.'

I had heard many stories about Sethu mash. When I asked Sunanda's sister where I could find him, she gave me directions to Surendran mash who she said knew Sethu mash. In fact, Surendran mash was not a Naxalite. He hadn't been arrested either. But he had checked into a mental asylum by the time the Emergency was lifted. It was unsettling to think that he'd still lose sleep on a piece of paper that Das had purportedly given him years ago. I too wished to see it. But in reality he had never been given any blueprint. Sethu mash confirmed that other than his delusion of its possession, there was no such document.

Sethu mash's house was close to the medical college. Walking along a narrow alley that barely allowed a bicycle to pass, I stopped in front of a tiled, small but neatly maintained house where I found Sethu mash chewing on a betel-leaf blend. He was wearing a flowing white khadi shirt that could have accommodated four more persons of his size. He laughed heartily. 'That is how fascism wins,' he said. 'The fascists scare people to their bones until they no longer want to be themselves. We all have a bit of a fascist in us, my friend. Take the example of a mother and her child. The mother does have a fascist strain in her. She wants her child to never leave her, love only her, and continue her lineage and so on.'

He laughed again, his whole body shaking along the length of his laughter. 'Just wait and watch. Do you see what is happening all around us? People have become thieves. The total worth of gangsters in our tiny state has crossed fifty thousand crore now. They produce illicit hooch, operate murder syndicates, and sell off girls . . . God save us!'

'Please talk to me about Das, mash?' I pleaded. 'Where is he? What illness does he have? I need to meet him. You have to help me, mash.'

Suddenly mash became silent. My voice cracked. My love for Yudas must have soaked my voice completely.

'I've got no one else, mash. My love for him began when I was fifteen. I could never forget him in this life. Mash, you must help me. Please make him understand. I want to live with him.'

'That is not possible, dear,' mash said. 'He wouldn't be able to. He has no deliverance from the past. For that matter, none of us do.'

I stubbornly insisted on meeting him.

He chewed some more betel leaves, laughing heartily. 'Let it go. Don't see him. He is no more. That's how you should think about him.'

I sat in front of him, frozen.

'My dear,' he continued, 'please go back, live happily and marry a good man who can take care of you very well. By the time you bear a couple of children, you will be cured of this ailment.'

'My ailment isn't likely to go away.' I was adamant. 'I have ulcers.'

'I didn't mean that,' mash said, laughing again, 'but the bug in your heart!' He then stood up to leave as I looked on. 'I am getting late. I have to attend a meeting at Kakkayam. Funeral rites for the Emergency are being held there! Let's not make folks grumpy just because I couldn't be there.'

'I too am coming,' I announced, wiping my face and springing to my feet. 'As long as you don't tell me where Das is, I will follow you wherever you go.'

Mash guffawed. 'Who said you couldn't? Come right along, my friend!'

Mash joked quite a lot during the journey. It was a good ride to Kakkayam. As soon as we passed Atholi, the topography began to change around us and the bus hustled faster. Ullieri, Naduvannur, Perambra . . . Benumbed, I leaned on the rails of the window to take in the experience of travelling to a mysterious world that belonged to another time. Mountains, farmlands, solitary stores . . . I felt dizzy when the bus manoeuvred wide turns.

Mash left his seat in the rear to sit beside me. 'Hey there, do you like the land?' he asked with a chuckle.

'Nice,' I said.

'Who says our cops don't have an eye for art, my friend?' he quipped. 'There couldn't have been a better location to kill off people, could there?'

That was true. The turns, twists, trees and flowers. Yudas began to hang rocks again on the tattered veins of my broken heart.

Mash took a deep breath before saying, 'They arrested me at night. Right before they caught the captain. My mother's condition was worsening by the hour. Someone in plain clothes visited us at night. He asked politely if I was at home. "There is a little problem, mash. Parameswaran Saar would like you to redress that." I understood what he meant. I asked him if I could give a drop of water to my mother. There was holy water from Ganga at home. I gave her two spoons of water. I told her softly, "Amma, we may not see each other again," as I planted a kiss on her forehead. I was sure of that. Was there any guarantee that I would be released ever? I prepared to go and sat in the vehicle. They took me to the office of the superintendent of police for interrogation. When it was dark outside, they covered my eyes and put me in a car. I do remember the twists, turns and potholes of these roads.' He stretched back on the seat and exhaled. 'To sit blindfolded in a vehicle is a terrible state to be in. You need to go through it to know it, my friend.'

I sat in silence. I could actually visualize that night. I was transported like a blind man accompanied by cops on either side. There was no mountain or valley, just the twists and turns. I was imagining the journey Yudas undertook. Lord! What must've gone through my precious Yudas's delicate mind as he made the trip with his eyes taped at such a young age? The Beast's story of twenty-four-hour interrogation flashed in my memory. It filled my heart with pride to know that Yudas had held out for as long as he possibly could. But he lost. Poor thing. Shouldn't a fighter have the choice to lose? As the bus crossed a river whose water had a slimy green hue, I suddenly sat up straight. The river had unsettling currents. Mash remarked that the shutters of the dam must have been opened. I stared at the green water. The colour must be more intense at the gorge. Sunanda's body could be recovered should someone dive into it. I remembered her face from the old black-and-white passport-size photo: wide-eyed, with a swagger in her demeanour, as if she was ready to dare someone. If someone were to drop deeper in the gorge, they would see her lying in the depths that way—eyes wide open, lips puckered halfway through a sardonic smile. Oh Liberty!

We got down at Kakkayam. It was a nondescript intersection. Four shops, a store selling chicken, a few snack bars and vegetable vendors. There were four or five people milling about in front of martyr Rajan's monument that was painted red. Someone was addressing the crowd with a microphone in his hand.

'Let's go, friend, time to listen to this fellow pissing through his mouth,' mash commented.

The speaker's topic was fascism.

'This guy's party is the biggest of all fascist outfits. Do they even care what they're doing on the throne of power?'

I asked if we could pay a visit to the infamous prison camp of Kakkayam.

'We're going to need permission for that,' mash answered. 'There is no camp any more. It is now a factory which belongs to a conglomerate.'

I really wanted to go. 'Let's go this one time, please?'

He agreed to my plea. We left the intersection to trek along the path towards the camp. We passed the crowd and speakers on our way uphill. I gasped for air as we climbed, overcome by fatigue. The road became steeper. To its right, wet clothes had been spread out to dry in the yards of a few houses. Red chillies too were laid out beside the clothes. Mash paused for a moment. 'These houses were here even then,' mash said. 'There were people here too. Perhaps a generation older. They'd come here to work at the dam.' A young woman who was watching over the chillies observed us with curiosity.

The path leading to the old camp was barricaded. Someone from the security post came out. 'What do you want?' he asked tersely. As soon as we told him that we were here to see the camp, he raged, 'Do you have permission? If not, you can't go.'

Mash smiled at me and exclaimed: 'You heard that? We need permission to move about in our own land.'

'This place belongs to the board, old man,'

'And whom does the "board" belong to? People, right? Or is this your father's property?'

'Don't get mad at me, old man. I will let you in if you have permission. If not, I can't.'

I grabbed mash's arm and said, 'Let it go, mash. We won't see it now. We can come back another day.' My body began to shake a little. I began to feel the agony which Yudas and Sunanda had been subjected to—I saw the windowpanes of the prison camp blocked off by blackened sheets of paper! The roller that was brought out of P.J. Thomas's household! The ceiling fans in the hallway that never stopped! In fear I watched the mountain ranges that'd echo if I'd screamed. I wanted to run away. I felt scared of the earth beneath my feet. The howling wind frightened me. The silence, the intense green foliage, the crepuscular sky and the numbing chill evoked a feeling of dread. I longed to meet Yudas.

My wheezing worsened as we descended. When we neared the house where the young woman was drying chillies, mash paused. 'Hey, let's stop here for a minute. I want to meet someone I know.' He walked towards the yard. 'Isn't this Ittichan's home? Is he around?'

The young woman stood up. 'My father is in bed. He is very ill.'

We entered the house. An emaciated aged man was lying on a bed made of coir. He asked in a tired voice: 'Who is it, girl?'

'I used to be in this camp, Ittichan. Do you remember me?' Sethu mash inquired.

'Who is this? Rajan?' he replied, shading his eyes with his hand. 'Heck, no! It can't be Rajan. Didn't he die? Didn't I go to court as a witness?'

My body shivered again. O Lord! I couldn't bear this torture from a bygone time any more. I smelled blood. 'Do you remember Das?' I asked. 'The one who tossed a girl's body into the gorge from Konippara ridge?'

The old man stared at me. He said, 'Not one, but two. A girl and a boy. I wasn't there. But I heard about it.'

'Why do you keep bringing up these things again and again, father?' The young woman from the front yard came inside the house. 'Didn't all that happen a very long time ago? It's all over! Could we just stop talking about it?'

'Pha! Shut your mouth,' the old man reproached the young woman angrily as he raised his head. 'You have to keep talking about them or such times will come back. Remind ourselves, and everyone, to talk about them— all the time. What do you know? We were all afraid even to step out in our own yard. There were cops everywhere. You could hear screams all the time from the camp a kilometre away. And what kind? Holy Spirit! Could a human bear those sounds ever?'

'Ittichan, you did carry me on your shoulders to the clinic,' Sethu mash said. 'Do you remember?'

'Don't I? Yes.' The old man laughed, baring his white teeth in his dark face. 'I do remember how you'd arrived. Like Gandhiji, helped on your way by cops on either side. One of them carried a cross of large bamboo poles on his shoulder. They brought you here on it, like Jesus Christ. Blood all over your body. All the youngsters who marched on their feet to the camp were brought back just like that— bloodied and tied to a pole. Do you know what they did to Rajan?'

'I don't want to hear it,' I said, 'I don't have the strength for it.'

The old man sighed. 'You folks don't have the strength to hear it? What about us? What about those who had to be there?'

Sethu mash smiled scornfully. 'What about us who had to suffer it? Let's go now, my friend,' he said, rising and turning towards me. Then he asked the old man, 'Haven't you been visited by print and television reporters to prey on old memories?'

'They have,' the old man grinned, 'but nobody is allowed here. I am not going to peddle my memories around, mash. I've got nothing left in this old age.'

Sethu mash pulled out a few rupee notes from his pocket to slip into the old man's hand. 'Take this, dear Ittichan. Get yourself some tobacco leaves.'

'Thunder in the spring!' Sethu mash was laughing hard as we left. 'The flowering trees in the spring of youth. How many of them did they lay to waste?'

I followed mash like a puppet.

'Where else do you want to go now?' he asked. 'Konippara ridge?'

I looked into mash's face. 'I need to see that gorge, mash, where Das tossed the bodies of Sunanda and her friend.'

Mash stopped walking. He stood motionless for a while. He wanted to say something, but the word seemed stuck in his throat. At last he lifted his left arm to my shoulder. Leaning on my shoulder, he walked with me a little farther.

'Das is in Chalakudy. Near a school by the river. You could go and meet him.'

We didn't talk any more. I boarded an early morning train to Chalakudy the next day. I asked around for a Yudas who recovered dead bodies from the river. An autorickshaw driver took me to him.

Yudas lived in a shanty near the riverbank. I found him some distance away, under a tree whose creepers had fallen into the running water. He was idly watching the currents. When he saw me walking down the bend, he tilted his face slightly. Yudas looked very different. The shirt he had on was tattered here and there. The hair was cropped off his face and head. His bristly face betrayed no emotions.

'I am back,' I announced provocatively.

He continued to hunch over, staring at his own hands. I sat beside him and rested my head on his shoulder. The green river flowed before us. The waves were fragile. A pebble would sink as soon as it was thrown into the diaphanous waters. I remembered the river in Kakkayam. The memory of its dense green waters and wild roars kept coming to me again and again.

'And you thought I would never find you again, Das?' I asked ruefully.

'Yu-Das,' he corrected.

His voice was cracked. I stretched my arms to caress his forehead, cheeks and neck. He'd be the only man for me to caress. But he remained motionless like a rock.

'What are you thinking about, Das?' I asked. 'How to give me the slip again?'

He tilted his face to look at me. 'I am not feeling well.'

'Don't you dive to recover bodies any more?'

'Yes.'

'Do you still lecture the boys from the shore on the art of love-making?'

His face turned crimson. I laughed hard.

'You are a coward.' I laughed again.

Das sat back as if he'd lost the argument. I told him that I'd been to Kakkayam, that I'd seen the river and the ridge of Konippara, and that I had goose pimples while walking on the same ground he trod on. Das looked at me, his head still tilted.

'Why do you keep walking on my trail again and again?'

'I don't know,' I said. 'I think of you when I get frightened.'

'Why do you get frightened, Prema?'

My voice got stuck in my throat. The breathlessness in this love had strangled my heart. I stood up helplessly.

'Come, let's go home,' he said. As soon as we got home, he lay down on the floor, on his back. 'I am not well, Prema,' he muttered. 'I have not been feeling well at all. I'll die soon. I am not going to be around when you come looking for me next time.'

My body convulsed, my blood surged. 'So?' I asked, seething with anger. 'So what?'

'I don't want you to come looking for me again.'

I peered at him for a while. 'I have no one else to go looking for.'

'I'm messed up. A good-for-nothing.'

'But I have great respect for you.'

'I've betrayed a movement . . . couldn't do justice to the trust a lady had in me.'

'Didn't the Beast—Officer Parameswaran—torture you for twenty-four hours? Yet you didn't utter a word. And if you did, it wasn't really your fault. You didn't betray anyone.'

'I did end up giving them her name.'

'Her name was on your lips out of love.'

'But that is how they got her.'

'Das,' I called him impatiently. 'I have been looking for you for the last five years. I have finally found you again. You will run away again, leaving me behind. I know. But please say something different this time! Anything! I'm tired of listening to you go on about Sunanda every time. Say something about me. Are those who were betrayed and thrown into a ravine the only people in this world? What about the rest of us who are tormented by the memory of it all?'

Agitated, I sat by Yudas's feet. After a little while he turned around to lay his head in my lap and stretched out again. That made me quiver. I wanted to cry. I ran my fingers through his hair. He looked at me.

'You are a beautiful woman, Prema,' he said. 'I've come to know about it only today!'

I felt like I needed to cry and laugh at the same time. 'If you'd really loved me, I would've become more beautiful.' I swallowed my pain.

He said, 'There is no value for beauty. The only thing that matters is strength. The strength to resist. One shouldn't bend, break or give up.' He stroked my cheeks and asked if he could go to sleep. Then he slept with his head on my lap. We stayed together like that for a long time. I dozed off after a while. When he moved, I hugged him tight and asked where he was going.

'I'll be back after a bath,' he said bashfully.

He pulled off his linens from the clothes line, put them in a bucket and left. I came out of the hut and watched as he walked towards the river. From where I stood, I saw him at a distance in the river. Dusk was settling. I couldn't understand why he had to go that far into the water. He was across the river now. Then it dawned on me. He had fooled me again. The river became desultory before the shore became empty. He had vanished into thin air. I stood in the abandoned hut, not knowing what to do. I waited there without sleeping a wink until daybreak. In the morning before I left the place, I opened the bag to pull out Sunanda's diary. I yanked the letter my father wrote to 'Beast' Parameswaran Sir.

My Lord and the Highest Honourable Parameswaran Sir

My Lord! I crumpled the letter and threw it into the river. I am committed to Yudas. The water would have to bring him back to me. I would allow only Yudas to make me his own.

EIGHT

It's not just the betrayer; his lover too is doomed to lose sleep.

I slept very little. I was in the hospital for many days. I thought about Yudas only when the red bitterness of blood oozed in my mouth. Blood found its way to my eyes as well. I kept searching for him wherever there was news of a death by drowning. I wrote sometimes to Sunanda's home to find out Yudas's whereabouts. I never got reliable information. However, when I read in one of the postcards that Yudas had visited Sangeeta, Sunanda's niece, my heart soared. But it sank again as soon as I read the rest of the letter.

He asked Sangeeta about you. You should meet Sangeeta when you have time. She is carrying a child now. People have called a strike opposing a brick kiln factory in her neighbourhood. She seems to have gone in the ways of her aunt. When you get a chance, Prema, please meet with her and advise her to be cautious. I lost the only sister I had. And now, if I were to lose the only daughter I have, how would I survive?

Disconcerted, I stared at the letter for a while. I felt fatigued and recharged at the same time. Revolutions do not cease. Little people persist with their might wherever they are.

Since I couldn't sleep in my hostel room, I pushed the window open to watch the night from my bed. I decided to meet Sangeeta as soon as I could. Yudas must be in the area. Each day my life was spiralling out of control, rotting like a piece of uneaten food. Sometimes it sank like a log in the rapids before it bobbed up again. Only my love for him burned like an undying ember in the hearth. My youth was evaporating like a can of water beaten down by the sun. My face lost its vigour and vitality and my skin lost its sheen and became shrivelled.

I'd been working as a clerk for an association of women in Kottayam. I'd got the job with the help of an old classmate's mother. It had been many years since I met Yudas.

Sangeeta's house was only a little far from the town of Thrissur. It rained a lot the day I arrived at her house. The region had country roads beneath a canopy of trees with dense green foliage and dark trunks. I felt a lightness walking alone on the road. I wished Yudas had been with me. If only we could walk under the rain without the weight of past! We could have chatted about the trees or flowers along the way; or laughed watching children zip past us on bicycles with umbrellas in the pouring rain! I craved for a hearty joke and a laugh. Our generation had lost the ability to look into each other's eyes to laugh and love. My father's generation had taken away even the gift of a guileless smile.

The rain-soaked walk led me into the middle of the band of protestors shouting slogans. Sangeeta emerged from the crowd with an open umbrella as soon as she saw me. She had a flowing long hair neatly plaited with thin strands taken from either side of her head. One end of her sari—black flowers printed on white—was tucked along her belly. The changes in the body and face of a demure, newlywed and pregnant girl were apparent. Her dark, oily and shiny face glowed with an uncommon light of bravery and resolve. 'Sister, I hope you didn't have too much trouble finding my place. Please come. My house is very close. Our strike has passed forty-five days today. Would you like tea?'

I looked at her while the rain streamed down my face and smiled. 'I don't need anything now. I came here to see you because of a letter from your mother. You look well.'

She blushed a little. 'I think Mother might not have told you this. I am pregnant.'

I kept gazing at her without batting an eyelid. The teenager whom I had met long ago was going to become a mother. A thought crossed my mind just then: What if Sunanda had lived? What if she were alive, married to Das and pregnant? My heart was heavy. I wouldn't have mattered in his life any more! My heart yearned to meet Yudas. I had to find him. I needed to make him my own. I must bear his child and smile in this rain under an umbrella.

The agitation became louder now.

'The mud from the farmlands is going to be dug out starting today, sister,' Sangeeta said. 'They dig up all our lands. But we won't back off until we put an end to this. One way or another. We need our lands to farm. We'll sow the seeds. We'll reap the harvest. Our cattle must have fields to graze on, and move about. Our wells must have water.'

I stood alongside Sangeeta on the edge of the road, close to the band of agitators. Presently a procession of cars arrived, among them the vehicles of the district collector and the superintendent of police. There was a sudden commotion. The collector and the police officer stepped out of the rear seats of their respective cars. They wore long pants and taut belts, but they had the swagger of feudal lords from olden times. Some in the group behind them rushed to hold umbrellas over their heads, exhibiting a servile reverence. The collector read something out loud from a paper.

I could barely hear anything in the din. But I could see the man's face, the muscles distended to their limits to give the impression of a rocky exterior on his fair-complexioned face. What troubled me was the scowl he sported as he faced a motley bunch of poor people shouting slogans. It betrayed his arrogance and hatred for them.

'The law is against you. You have to submit to the court order,' the collector announced. The crowd became silent. 'We have to fulfil our duties. The court has ordered us to provide protection to the factory owners. You need to disperse, immediately.'

All of a sudden, Sangeeta, who'd been standing next to me, hurled her umbrella away and strode towards the crowd. I was stunned to see her push the crowd aside and confront the collector. 'Mr Collector!' I heard her razor-sharp voice clearly. 'Tell us how we—about two hundred and fifty poor people—shall live? Where should we go for water when the wells have been dried up?' The collector stared at her contemptuously. But she wasn't done yet: 'Mr Collector, don't forget the meaning and purpose of your position. It is not meant to serve only the rich, but to serve common people.'

The collector glowered at her as his face reddened.

'The factory owners too have the same rights as you,' he blurted out.

Sangeeta exploded in fury. 'Aren't you ashamed of yourself, sir, to say this to my face? One of the owners is a close relative of your uncle, isn't he? That man is a millionaire. Does he really need to uproot the livelihood of these poor folks just to dig up a little more wealth?'

The crowd began to stir while I looked on in bewilderment. Sangeeta was shoved back—it may have been the cops. I too jumped in without even realizing what I was doing. Suddenly, the situation became tense. The officers were mobbed by the agitators. The police charged at the crowd with batons. People ran helter-skelter. When I turned, a cop was viciously kicking a fallen Sangeeta. I discarded my bag and the umbrella and threw myself between them. I received a few blows and jabs, but I was able to rescue her. After most of the mob had been forced to flee, the police tossed Sangeeta, me and a few others into the jeep and drove us to the station. There, they registered a case against all of us and then let us go.

The rain had completely stopped when we left the police station. However, the leaves on the trees were still wet with raindrops. I scolded Sangeeta for behaving so irresponsibly in her condition. She listened with a warm smile, as we walked together. After I was done, she turned towards me.

'I am not scared, sister,' she said, 'Don't I have the blood of my aunt Sunanda and my grandfather coursing through me?'

I was speechless. My blood froze—the blood of my father. I felt like I had been defeated for a moment. Rage surged inside me. Sunanda was always ahead of me.

The agitators had declared that they would fast unto death. They built a makeshift shelter to continue the strike. That night Sangeeta took me to her modest house where she served me rice porridge and hot boiled tapioca in a plate made of clay. The rice, harvested from their own field, looked like the rosy fingertips of newborn babes. I was impatient to ask her about Yudas, but I didn't get an opportunity as I listened to Sangeeta's rant about the strike.

'Poor people don't deserve to live, do they? That is what the rich barons want. If there are no poor, how will the rich live? All by themselves? I don't understand, sister, I am frightened by man's capacity for greed and deception. What kind of world is this? Think of my little one who is about to be born into this wreckage!'

She left me at home and returned to the location of the strike. I couldn't sleep at all. I tossed and turned on the bed made with unwashed sheets. I'd decided to find out about Yudas sometime tomorrow. I would not let him go this time. The next morning, I woke up only after Sangeeta's husband came and knocked on the door. Panic struck me when he asked for Sangeeta. He too became alarmed when I told him that Sangeeta had gone back to the agitators' late in the night. He said Sangeeta hadn't come to the strike shelter last night.

It was a bleak dawn. We ran in all directions in search of her. The endless field was empty and silent. Our calls of 'Sangeeta' echoed eerily. Finally, someone found a plastic slipper in a gorge that had been mined deep for clay to bake bricks. The ravine was an unsightly spectacle; the crowd remarked that it was at least thirty or forty feet deep. Cattle usually drowned in there. I felt a chill racing down my spine. Tremors shook my whole body—it was not under my control any more. The possibility that Sangeeta could be following Sunanda's fate hit me hard. History had begun to repeat itself, and I was desperate to get out of there.

Sangeeta's husband bawled from the edge of the field. He attempted to jump into the gorge, but some in the crowd pulled him back. Nobody had dared to dive into the gorge. I hung around, not knowing what to do. Suddenly, I tucked the loose end of my sari into my waist, gathered my hair into a bun and sashayed from the elevation of the field into the gorge. I couldn't help but remember a fifteen-year-old from another time, long long ago, who had run from Yudas's home to throw herself into the lake. This wasn't the same. A gorge isn't a lake. I sank right into it. My white-dotted red cotton sari unfurled on the surface of the water like an umbrella. Someone in the crowd hollered. I didn't pay attention. I had entered the water after a long time. The water received my quivering body warmly and I submitted myself to it. It had the odour of mud. The water beneath the meadows drew me in like a yawning well or a boundless tunnel. I felt blood ooze out of the ulcer wounds in my stomach. All the organs unhinged themselves within my body. Blood spurted as though it had come out of a newly dug well. The sour gooey blood filled my mouth.

I sank deeper into the water. I frantically reminded myself of Yudas. I loved him. I would go on loving him. Even at that moment when fluids were beginning to explode out of me through my lungs and heart, I longed for him intensely. How warm was the hearth of his chest. I could feel the same warmth from the water in the gorge. The vision of Sunanda drowning in the slimy green reservoir at Kakkayam came back to me again. I must be sinking in the same manner. The pressure from the water shot up by each passing moment. I pushed downwards obstinately. Deeper! I commanded myself. This ravine, this one that is thirty feet deep, is mine. As my respiratory organs dilated to their limits, a sharp pain began to seep in. I couldn't feel my limbs any more. I remembered Yudas. I remembered Sunanda. I remembered the youngsters from Kakkayam whom I hadn't heard or met and I remembered the machinery of the state and the tools that crushed them to oblivion.

This was my revolution, I thought to myself. I wasn't sure whom it was against. Perhaps against the collectors and the police superintendents with ruddy faces who had never had to walk under a harsh hot sun in their lives? Or against the wealthy factory owners who had surpassed the limits of greed to dig, dig and dig dirt from the fields only to burn it to death so that he could fill their deep pockets? Or perhaps this was against history herself. It must be against myself too. The gorge was as dark as the room whose windows were sealed tight with blackened sheets of paper. The darkness thickened as I sank further. The hum in my ears became louder. Someone whispered in my mind that it was the fans at the IB office. I caught the sound of someone's sobs. Beyond the layers of the past, from the valleys of Konippara hill to the roars of distant waterfalls, a thousand men and women were bellowing. I kept sinking amid the clamour of unrecognizable voices.

At last I caught hold of long hair! I pulled it towards me with all my strength. She sprang up. Her face shone slowly in the glow from the water. It seemed like she had a scornful smile on her face as she lay at the bottom of the gorge, on her back with crossed arms tucked underneath her head. I began to bawl. My hands and legs started to unwind. My lungs, heart and belly melted into the water. My eyes closed. Tugging at her stiff, frozen and lifeless body, I strained to yell: 'Sangeeta!'

I heard a call back to me:

Oh, Liberty what crimes are committed in thy name . . .

Oh, Liberty!

Images of Sunanda and Yudas flooded my mind. I fell into a fit of rage and despair. Sunanda kept coming back. She had stolen Yudas away from me. He'd never love me. I knew my strength was gone. I preferred to die in the gorge next to Sangeeta. Only then would Yudas love me. He was nothing more than a dreamer. He could only love martyrs, the kind who were dead, who never did anything worthwhile, whose ribs had been smashed to smithereens at the merciless hands of mindless officers like my father.

When I regained my senses, I was lying in the field like a wet piece of cloth. A short distance away I saw some people trying to straighten Sangeeta's lifeless body. Her husband's cries echoed over the fields. Sangeeta too was gone now. I was the only one alive, I thought. I convulsed in a sudden spasm. Blood and churned-up mud came gushing out of my mouth.

The crowd carried Sangeeta and me to a hospital. By the time I was discharged after receiving primary medical care, Sangeeta's asthmatic mother had arrived, having waded through the steep meadow and dreary fields. As soon as she saw me, she began to wail, 'Isn't she on her way to her aunt, Prema? Isn't she?'

I silently embraced her. She thanked me every now and then, occasionally extolling the virtues of her daughter between whimpers. Sangeeta's dead body had blue bruises. The post-mortem report confirmed that she hadn't died by drowning. She'd been thrown into the water only after she was dead. Telltale signs of brutal torture and unspeakable suffering were visible all over her body. Her breasts and thighs bore marks of severe whacks; her left shoulder and head revealed signs of multiple strikes by a blunt weapon. Somebody whispered that the owners of the brick kiln might be responsible; or perhaps the cops; or maybe even the collector who looked like he had never touched dirt in his life!

When the body was brought back after the post-mortem, it was greeted with a heart-wrenching wail. 'Sunandaaae!' Sangeeta's mother appeared to have lost her senses. She began to cry, hollering 'Sunanda'. She cursed and dared Indira Gandhi to declare the Emergency again. She threatened to kill Jayaram Padikkal, the police officer. She banged her head on the floor until she collapsed from exhaustion. Thereafter she woke up every now and then and bawled.

Still reeling from almost drowning in the gorge, I could only sit like a pillar. I didn't have the strength to move or even talk. Every time I thought about the gruesome manner of Sangeeta's death, I had seizures. My mouth tasted bitter blood.

People poured in to see the dead body. I haughtily held my head up to see if the possessor of any pair of feet was Yudas. Sangeeta's death had transformed me into another person. I wouldn't bow before Yudas any more. I had repaid his debt. I had taken back what he'd given to the gorge. Proved that I had the courage for a revolution and that I could keep secrets. Yet I was alive. In this world, for poor people like us, oughtn't the sheer act of being alive be counted as a revolution in itself?

NINE

A traitor cannot settle down anywhere. He'll be a renegade everywhere. His lover too won't have a place of her own.

On the fourth day after Sangeeta's death, an unexpected event occurred that turned my life upside down. I was feeding Sunanda's mother a bit of hot porridge at night by the light of the sole chimney lamp in the house. I was wiping away the trickling porridge from the corner of her lips when a boy from the agitators' group came running past the hill and fields towards the house.

'Sister, you've got to get out! Right now! Let's go!'

I didn't understand anything. Even as I wondered where I could go, he pulled me up by my hand. 'Maoists have been captured. The cops will try to frame you as a Maoist. They are preparing to arrest you. If you surrender, you are a goner. That'll be the end.'

I was aghast. My hair stood on end. I was about to be arrested . . . for having taken part in a revolution. My veins throbbed. My blood warmed up. For the first time in my life, I wanted to burst out laughing. My day had arrived. It'd be right here that I'd get to yell in the cops' faces: 'Long Live the Revolution, you mongrels.'

'Sister, let's get going—right now! We don't have much time to spare. Let's find you a shelter before the night is over! Imagine if we were to get caught!'

He was the one to find my leather bag and shove all my clothes into it. He didn't even let me wash my hands. He simply threw away the plates and started running across the fields, towing me along. It was a cold night. The roads were slippery and I tripped a few times in the darkness. But I kept laughing all the way and he kept reminding me that the police was after us. I ran, heaving breath into my lungs, spitting out blood from the ulcers in my mouth every now and then. I sprinted merrily. The passion and exhilaration of the fifteen-year-old girl who rushed out of Yudas's shack surged within me again. Struggling to catch my breath, I called out as I ran, 'Naxalbari Zindabad. Total Revolution Is Our Goal, Future Generations Belong to Us. Martyrs Zindabad . . .'

We ran until he reached some distance beyond the expansive field, crossing an alley and a bridge. He put me in a taxi there for the rest of the journey. The taxi avoided all the main roads to manoeuvre its way around. I lowered the window by the rear seat and enjoyed the nippy breeze, smiling as the night darkened outside. I must have dozed off in the car midway through the journey. When I opened my eyes we'd already arrived in Kumarakom, far away in the south.

'Why are we here?' I asked in surprise.

'This is the place,' said the old taxi driver.

Parking the car in front of one of the shuttered shops, he got out to survey the location. When he had made sure the area was safe, he instructed me to come out of the car. We walked briskly by the shoreline of a lake.

Green frogs leapt across our path, cutting off the tiny light from the pencil torch that guided us. A rooster crowed ominously above our heads. The warm breeze from the lake accompanied us. I felt relieved and happy. Finally we saw a slender but long beam of light falling on the lake from a chimney lamp. The driver headed in that direction. It was the beached wreckage of a boat whose top had a tarpaulin cover. From a distance I could see an angler perched on the other end of the boat that led into the lake. As I neared the boat, my limbs froze. I knew who it was—Yudas!

I stood motionless even after the driver asked me to step inside. Yudas brought the lamp to get a closer look at us. I will not forget the moment when the light from that chimney lamp fell on my face until my dying breath. My hair stood on end as the warm yellow glow caressed me. Creasing his forehead to take a better look, he came closer to me and called out in surprise, 'Oh! Prema!'

This time I couldn't talk to him like I used to when he would inquire about my whereabouts. He gently offered me a hand to lead me inside the boat. He gave me water from a clay pot which I gulped to quench my thirst. He had put on some weight. The bags under his eyes were red and sagging. In the yellow light his body looked like a cadaver that had been laid in the water for many days. Seeing his condition reminded me of the passage of time and it tore at my heart. I tried hard to hold back my tears. He seemed happier than I had thought he would be on our meeting.

'I have been thinking about you,' he said. He had seen the driver off and now we were walking to the thatched corner of a ramshackle house nearby.

'That's good.'

'You must be mad at me.'

'For what?'

'Don't be angry at me, Prema. You shouldn't curse me either.'

He spoke as if this was a regular conversation. I felt like crying. His room looked the same as all the other rooms he had inhabited everywhere else. The clothes line had towels with red dirt stains. The room was filled with the odour of moisture.

'You look so different now, Prema,' he said as he unfurled a straw mat for me to sit down upon.

'I am getting on in age. Aren't I?'

'In my mind, you are still that fifteen-year-old girl. You were always so stubborn.'

'In my mind you are still that old "Croc" Yudas.' I peered at him in fatigue. 'Do you still pull dead bodies out of water?'

Yudas's face turned pale. He didn't answer that question.

'You still don't like to talk about it, do you?' I inquired, drawing satisfaction from my ruthlessness.

'Nothing like that.'

He pulled out a beedi tucked in a plastic cover and lit it. The room was filled with the pungent oppressive smell of ganja.

He said, 'There isn't much to talk about. Is there?'

'Isn't there?' I asked vengefully. 'I thought that is the only thing you could really say something about.'

Yudas looked at me with a tired face. 'You are upset with me, Prema. Aren't you?'

'I love you.'

He was flustered.

'I thought about that,' he said. 'And I haven't been able to get that. Why do you love me?'

'Why do you recover dead bodies?'

He didn't respond.

'Do you still yell "Long Live the Revolution, mongrels!" when you bring bodies back?'

He laughed timidly. 'Sometimes. It's just a habit.'

'How about "Victory to Naxalbari"?'

'That too is no more than a habit.'

'Loving you is the same for me. A habit.'

I wiped away my tears with a corner of my sari. I was exhausted. I am almost thirty-six now. Thirty years after the Emergency, I thought to myself. Thirty years after Kakkayam. I can't take it any more. I am tired. Yudas is ageing.

'I am an old man now,' Yudas said, throwing away the beedi he had been taking long drags from. 'Time to let go of everything.'

I fell asleep watching him. When I woke up, my stomach was burning. The pain of the ulcers flared again. Solitary frogs croaked in the swamp. The day passed very quickly. By dusk he appeared to have become a little weaker. He repeated a few times how he hadn't expected me to be the night-time visitor.

'So were you mad or sad when you came to know it was me?' I asked feistily.

'I am not going to argue with you, Prema.'

'Oh! Do I need to argue with you now? What ruse do you have this time to run away from me? I've paid your debt. You threw Sunanda into a gorge. I recovered her niece from another.'

Rage filled my body and I felt blood in my mouth.

'I can't do this any more, Yudas. There is no more debt to repay.'

Yudas sat motionless, silent.

'You are right,' he whispered at last. 'There is no more debt.'

Tears welled up in my eyes.

'I have nowhere to go . . . I will not let you get away from me either. I am almost thirty-six years old now. I have been chasing you since I was fifteen. I am tired of it. I don't think I will live much longer . . .'

My voice cracked. He kept gazing at me.

'Prema, that . . . No . . . That won't work . . .'

'I lost my beauty, my youth . . . All gone! You don't even want to see my face . . . That is why you stay away from me . . . You've never even loved me . . .' I blurted out addressing no one in particular. Yudas's eyes became moist. He came and sat next to me.

'You are a good girl. I am an old man, aren't I? A fifty-year-old man. I can only ruin your life, along with mine.'

'I don't care.'

'Are you crazy?'

I suddenly laughed and leaned on his chest.

'Long Live the Revolution . . .' I said.

He hugged me, drawing me close.

'You are still a child.'

I laughed, resting my cheek on his chest. My eyes were damp again.

'This world needs us.'

He didn't say anything. He just kept looking at me with compassion. Dusk was settling outside. My love for him grew stronger. Being a virgin at the age of thirty-six could only mean stupidity. He was my man. I was tired of hauling this ageing body like a crocodile trudging along the shore.

'Sometimes I feel like I should die,' I told him. 'When I die, it should be by drowning. And you ought to be the one to recover my body. That is my only wish.'

'Stop talking crazy, Prema.'

He stood up and began pacing back and forth in distress. I rested my chin on my knees and watched him from where I sat on the mat. When I asked if he was still lecturing local boys on love-making, he smiled apologetically. Then he pulled out a bottle of liquor, downed a couple of gulps, and served me a plateful of cold rice and gravy which he may have cooked before noon. I ate it with tears in my eyes. It felt like the last supper. After dinner I lay down with my head on his lap as I had always done.

'Please don't leave me behind,' I pleaded with him.

'You should stop loving me.'

This time he didn't cry, but his voice broke.

After a long time the chimney lamp in the room went out suddenly. The yellow lights of the houseboats flickered in the distance. He began to speak in a whimpering voice. 'You haven't figured me out. You don't see my heart.

I am a prisoner of my memories for life. There is no escape for me. It is a camp for torture. You don't know, Prema, but my memories have been brutalizing me. I don't have any respite from them. I have betrayed. I can't take back the secrets I divulged. I am cursed, Prema. You cannot love someone like me. They beat Sunanda to pulp. Her voice still echoes in my ears. She never cried. When the pain became unbearable, she would heave a little. At other times she would grunt. She was at war with herself. What courage she had! I have not seen a woman like her since.'

I was distraught. 'You have no eyes to see who I am,' I complained.

'You aren't like that,' he was saying. 'A little child. You have the heart of a flower. She was just the opposite. An iron rod. She didn't bend even when she was on molten fire. You never saw her face. You never saw the face that clenched down insufferable pain. Lord! How could I betray her? How could I even point my finger at her? I shouldn't have given her up even at the cost of my own life. What kind of a man am I? Was I ever one? I am a beast. Or the devil. You don't know. I haven't been able to kill my hunger ever since, nor quench my thirst. I need to drink water all the time. I have tried to immerse myself in the lake to drink water to at least wet my throat. But no. My throat doesn't even feel it. The drought in my mouth doesn't end. It is an unbearable state to be in. That is why I keep drinking alcohol. When I do, deep in my throat, there is a burning sensation. As if it is on fire. Let my gasping throat scorch in the fire. After we were tortured, I'd feel the same burning sensation when I urinated. Did you know that when you are beaten from head to toe, urine doesn't come out of your body, instead you pee blood. Thick red blood.'

Lying on his chest, I had the salty taste of blood in my mouth. A whimper sprang up in my heart again. 'To hell with fascism,' I said. 'Total Revolution Is Our Goal.'

He tightened his arms around me.

'My poor little girl. It feels like I may have betrayed you too. I shouldn't have, no?'

'Why did you come to my village?' I asked.

'I had no real destination. I was on the road for a long time. I liked the lake when I saw it and I stopped there. I could only live in the vicinity of water. I've lost many things in my life to water, things that were dearest to me. I have to recover them. I'll dive in every cranny to get them back for the sake of the world.'

His voice cracked. I noticed his heartbeats didn't have the old timbre any more. I could clearly make out the broken tenor. I asked if he had ever gone back to Kakkayam.

Unsettled, he blurted out, 'Me? Again in this life?'

'I did. I took everything you flung away in the gorge. Now we must go there together, for no particular reason.' I pulled him closer to me. Perhaps these knots that constricted us would unwind by themselves.

I spoke to Yudas about my father. About how he had even begun to lose his ability to talk. I recalled those times when he had roared 'BLOODY ROTTEN SCUM OF AN ASS-IMPALER' and hurled my mother and me by our hair. I spoke about 'Beast' Parameswaran and the letter my father had written to him.

Yudas was sympathetic. 'Some folks are like that,' he said. 'Ear-splitting screams of pain from a fellow human give them a thrill. Spilling others' blood excites them.' His eyes welled up and he continued, 'I remember the face of a policeman who pierced nails into the inmates' fingers. He'd try so hard to contain his potbelly as he went down on his knees. He took the greatest care when drilling nails through each finger. You should have seen the fury and frustration on his face should the inmate's body jerk and recoil. Most of them came to torture us in a semi-conscious state after getting drunk. They were like automatons. It was hard to believe all of those things that happened. Not any more though.'

He lay his head in my lap and watched me, his eyes shining in the murky light. I felt as though my chest which had been under a spell of great drought for years had suddenly cooled. He had never shown such intimacy towards me until now. I was blissfully imagining that he would finally take me as his woman. We had shared something; a give-and-take was happening between us. I laughed merrily like a fifteen-year-old. I empathized with my old feudal Naalukettu at the same time. It could while its time for a little longer. Or my younger brother could offer it to the Pentecostals for their charismatic prayers. Believers in their sufferings would speak in tongues; retell holy witnesses; cry and holler begging God's mercy. I'd amused myself imagining what it would be like if my father were to live in that time in the future. God might bless my father with another opportunity to hear screaming human beings to his heart's fill. He may be baptized in the water at the lake—in the impervious slimy green water. I probed Yudas's dishevelled ochre locks with my fingers to caress them. The memories of water in the lake Yudas and I swam in had warmed my heart. The same water from where he pulled me up like a kingfisher yanking out a pearl fish. Yudas slowly closed his eyes, and I watched him slide into sleep involuntarily.

I empathized with myself and Yudas. We were just two ill-fated people. I gently stroked his chest. His chest was covered in blood clots. Every time he inhaled, his groans became louder. If he went back deep in the water, he wouldn't be able to hold his breath for long any more. The water thrust with greater pressure with each passing year. The force from the pressure could pin him down and crush his ribcage in the end. He might lose all his strength and fall apart. The fire in a defeated warrior would never die out. His ribcage would not have known what leisure was. The burning hearts of those who fell in love with the vanquished would never cool.

I stayed awake, watching over Yudas. He would slip away if I slept even for a moment. How many more years would I have to wander to find him again? How many more reservoirs would he have to swim, flailing in his attempts to recover what he lost in the water? My lake was lucid. The dusk had showered it with gold coins minted from sunbeams. Moonlight had poured molten diamonds into it. A trove of enigmatic secrets lay snuggled in the lake's depths, tucking their flaps above their heads, beneath the nests of grinning chromides.

I will take him to my shore when he wakes up. In the agony borne out of broken ribcages, who knows if it will be he or I who tosses the other into the lake. One of us would have to be on the lookout to dive and recover the dead body. When the body, bitten by fish into a human coral, arrives at the bank, one would have to stay awake in order to drape the dead in white clothes and burn incense sticks.

One of us, or perhaps all of us.

~ ~ ~

ACKNOWLEDGEMENTS

It was during a women writers' meeting in Delhi, while waiting to listen to the famous Gloria Steinem, that my dear friend and noted Malayalam poet Anita Thampi touched the core of this novel in one sentence. 'I have heard of a Naxalite who suffers from the crushing guilt of outing what he knew when the police brutalized him.' She didn't say anything more. But in that one moment, I had experienced this book. Although I didn't write the book until several months later, I am grateful for that one line and the friendship that has lasted till date.

There are not enough words to thank Madhu Mash, theatre activist, who shared memories of the Emergency and accompanied me to Kakkayam, and K. Venu, former Naxal leader and social activist for the slogans used in this book.

After the publication of *Hangwoman*, the translation of *Aarachar*, R. Sivapriya, then commissioning editor at Penguin, had asked about my next book. My dear friend Dr Piyush Antony and her brother Dr Amal Antony have always wanted to see 'Yudasinte Suvisesham'— Gospel of Yudas—in English. I suggested Yudas to Siva and she immediately commissioned the book and handed it over to Ambar Sahil Chatterjee. Thank you, Siva, Piyush and Dr Amal.

I haven't met Rajesh Rajamohan in person yet; we only spoke over the phone. Rajesh took time out of his busy schedule to work on the book only out of his love for the art of translation. Heartfelt gratitude to Rajesh for having recreated Yudas's and Prema's travails in English.

The book was made possible on schedule only due to the efforts of my editor Ambar, who became a close friend in a very short time. My dear Ambar, thank you so much!

I am yet to meet Shatarupa Ghoshal in person. She was the copy editor for *Hangwoman* too. My words, despite being in the garb of another language, are safe in her hands. Thank you, Shatarupa.

The creators of the book's incredible cover are Meena Rajasekharan, the cover designer, and Ranganath Krishnamani, the illustrator. My heartfelt gratitude to them.

My special thanks to Prasad Lakshmanan, the editor of *Kalakaumudi*, who published 'Yudasinte Suvisesham' in its entirety; my dear friend P. Muraleedharan; and S.P.C.S, the publishers.

GLOSSARY

Incha: A natural substitute for artificial toilet soaps, traditionally used for bathing after oil massage. It is extracted from the bark of the forest climber *Acacia intsia*.

Mash: A teacher; a respected person.

Naalukettu: A traditional Kerala house with a central courtyard, where rich upper-caste feudal lords lived.

ABOUT THE AUTHOR AND
THE TRANSLATOR

K.R. Meera made her mark in Malayalam journalism in 1998 when she won the prestigious Journalism for Human Rights award instituted by the People's Union of Civil Liberties for an investigative series on the plight of women labourers in Kerala. Later she won the Chowara Parameswaran Award instituted by the Kerala Press Academy, the Deepalaya Child Rights Award and the British Chevening Scholarship for Young Indian Print Journalists, 2005. She quit her job to become a full time writer in 2006.

Meera began writing fiction in 2001. Her first collection of short stories, *Ormayude Njarampu* (2002), won several prestigious awards, including the Ankanam Sahithya Award, Lalithambika Antharjanam Award for young writers, the Geetha Hiranyan Endowment Award of the Kerala Sahitya Akademi and the Thrissur Kerala Varma Katha Award. Her second collection of short stories, *Moha Manja*, won the E.V. Krishna Pillai Smaraka Piravi Award. Her short novel *Karineela* won the Thoppil Ravi Smaraka Katha Award. Her short story *Guillotine* won the P. Padmarajan Award and the V.P. Sivakumar Memorial Keli Award in 2008. *Ave Maria* won the Kerala Sahitya Akademi Award for the best short story collection published during 2006–08. She was shortlisted for the Confederation of Tamil Nadu Malayali Associations (CTMA) Literary Prize in 2012. *Aarachar* won the Nooranad Haneef Memorial Novel Award in 2013, the prestigious Odakkuzhal Award, the coveted Vayalar Ramavarma Award along with the Kerala Sahitya Akademi Award for the best novel in 2014 and the Kendra Sahitya Akademi Award for the best novel in Malayalam in 2015.

Yellow Is the Colour of Longing, the translation of the story *Moha Manja* by J. Devika was selected as one of the three stories representing South Asia by the prestigious feminist journal *Feminist Review* published from London. In 2011 Penguin India brought out a collection of fifteen short stories by Meera, titled *Yellow Is the Colour of Longing* (translated by J. Devika) which was shortlisted for the Economist-Crossword Translation Prize.

Hangwoman (2014), the translation of *Aarachar* by J. Devika, published by Penguin India in 2014, has received rave reviews from national media and critics. The novel found place in several Best of Fiction 2014 lists across the media and was also shortlisted for the DSC Literature Prize 2016.

Aa Maratheyum Marannu Marannu Njan was translated by J. Devika and published by Oxford University Press in 2015 as *And Slowly Forgetting That Tree*.

Meera's stories have been rendered into Tamil, Telugu, Kannada and Hindi also.

She lives in Kottayam with husband M.S. Dileep, a journalist, and their daughter, Shruthi.

~ ~ ~

Rajesh Rajamohan has been working in the IT industry for almost two decades. He has translated *Litanies of Dutch Battery*, a major work of fiction by N.S. Madhavan, which won the Vodafone-Crossword Prize for Best Translated Fiction in 2011, and was shortlisted for The Hindu Literary Prize and longlisted for the Man Asian Literary Prize the same year. He has translated other works like *Karmayogi*, the widely acclaimed biography of E. Sreedharan. Rajesh lives in Pennsylvania, USA with his family.

ALSO BY THE SAME AUTHOR

Hangwoman
Translated by J. Devika

'A contemporary masterpiece'—*Mint*

The Grddha Mullick family bursts with marvellous tales of hangmen and hangings in which they figure as eyewitnesses to the momentous events that have shaped the history of the subcontinent. When twenty-two-year-old Chetna Grddha Mullick is appointed the first woman executioner in India, assistant and successor to her father, her life explodes under the harsh lights of television cameras. When the day of the execution arrives, will she bring herself to take a life?

Meera's spectacular imagination turns the story of Chetna's life into an epic and perverse coming-of-age tale. The lurid pleasures of voyeurism and the punishing ironies of violence are kept in agile balance as the drama hurtles to its inevitable climax.

'Meera weaves history, romance and the politics of the present together into a narrative of incredible complexity'—*Caravan*

'Immense, intense . . . [with] chillingly clear-eyed vignettes . . . [and] moments of razor-sharp dark humour too'—*India Today*

'One of the most extraordinary accomplishments in recent Indian fiction'—*Indian Express*

'A daring book . . . Deliciously engrossing'—*The Hindu*

'An epic novel'—*Outlook*